Young, Gifted, and Rich

The Secrets of America's Most Successful Entrepreneurs

by Ralph Gardner, Jr.

A Wallaby Book
Published by Simon & Schuster, Inc.
New York

For my parents

Published by Wallaby Books
A Division of Simon & Schuster, Inc.
Simon & Schuster Building
1230 Avenue of the Americas
New York, New York 10020

Designed by Judy Allan (The Designing Woman)

WALLABY and colophon are registered trademarks
of Simon & Schuster, Inc.

First Wallaby Printing April 1984
10 9 8 7 6 5 4 3 2 1

Manufactured in the United States of America
Printed and bound by Fairfield Graphics

Library of Congress Cataloging in Publication Data

Gardner, Ralph.
    Young, gifted, and rich.

    1. Businessmen—United States—Biography.   2. Capital-
ists and financiers—United States—Biography. I. Title.
HC102.5.A2G37   1984   338′.04′0922 [B]   83-26018
ISBN 0-671-47046-9

Acknowledgments

Thanks to Gene Brissie for his encouragement; to Melissa Newman for her excellence as an editor; to my cousin Paul Wachter for having such young, gifted, and good friends, and for introducing them to me.

Thanks also to Mickey and Jessica Mayerson for letting a stranger stay in their home in Los Angeles; to Paul Chiten for letting me sleep on his waterbed in Berkeley; and especially to Debbie Downing for her friendship.

Contents

Introduction

I've been asked what traits the people I profiled have in common. All have a relentless commitment to the process of creation, to building something great, rather than to the material rewards of their success. As Jean Yates explained, "The thing I like about this job is not the money. If you like the money and you like the prestige and you like the trappings, you'll never make it. What you have to like is the process. You have to like the agony of building it."

All the people profiled here were able to discipline themselves into working hard and well. As unsensational as it may sound, plain hard work was the single most important factor in their success. It's the kind of discipline that makes little kids cry and adolescents rebel when their parents force it on them. These people force it on themselves. I've never met a group of people who worked harder. I would guess they average about five hours of sleep a night.

All of them have vision. By vision I don't mean that they fantasize delivering the State of the Union Address twenty years down the road. Rather, they have a vision of excellence and they know when they're producing it. The number of cookie stores Debbie Fields owns or the number of computers Steve Jobs sells is a by-product of that vision. It's not the vision itself.

All of them have bedrock confidence in their uniqueness and their ability to change the world. From this self-confidence flows courage, and from courage a willingness to take risks. I was surprised to see how little luck had to do with their success. I think what is usually termed "luck" is the subtle skill of seizing opportunity.

After almost two decades during which our whole culture seemed paralyzed by self-doubt, these young entrepreneurs are astonishingly free of insecurity or embarassment about making money. They are capitalists to the core. Even those who admit to having been hippies ten years ago unabashedly embrace capitalism as the way of nature.

If we're living in an age of limitations and reduced opportunities, that news has not yet reached these people. Though they come from many diverse groups—rich and poor, male and female, black and white, Ivy League educated and self-educated—they share a sense of unlimited opportunity.

My goal in each chapter was to convey the personality, the environment, the energy of the person I profiled. Some were willing to discuss the most private aspects of their lives. Others put up public relations facades. But in most cases I believe I captured the personality they projected to the world, the personality that helped them succeed.

During the interviews, I continually asked myself, What motivates these people? How do you account for their drive? After attempting to answer those questions, I don't dare generalize about motivation. It is profoundly personal, born in the crucible of circumstance and creative reaction that forms a human being. These are fifteen individuals with fifteen individual motivations.

Something that's certain is that once they've tasted success it acts like an amphetamine. It injects them with adrenalin that makes them demand more of themselves and everybody around them.

This is not a "How-To" book. None of the people I profiled got where they are by imitating anybody else. The reason they succeeded is because they believed they were special. They are.

Steve Jobs

Steve Jobs *might have drunk less wine, gotten to bed be-*fore 2:00 A.M., and not worn jeans and sandals to work, if he'd remembered he was supposed to meet a reporter at 9:00 A.M. and address something called the World Affairs Council at noon. But probably not. Part of being the symbol of the new age—which Steve is as the twenty-eight-year-old founder and chairman of the board of Apple Computers—is being able to spin visions of the future even when you've had a late night.

When he arrives at Apple headquarters in Cupertino, California, forty-five minutes late for his first meeting, he seems instantly in command. A company PR man is waiting in his office to brief him on the World Affairs Council and to assure him that it will take no more than fifteen minutes of his time.

Steve is simultaneously a PR man's dream and nightmare. He is smart, quick, and compelling enough to seduce any audience when he wants to. On the other hand, he might choose not to show up at all. It's one of the perks of unbounded power. "It could have been miserable," one of Steve's secretaries told me in relief after my interview went smoothly. "He might not even have seen you."

"He's incredibly bright and incredibly charming, just a delightful guy," an industry analyst said. "But walking around like a guru all the time isn't very good for character development."

Today Steve is on his best behavior. He doesn't need to be briefed on what to say to the political leaders at noon. "I'm supposed to talk about how the Japanese are not a terrible threat to the high-tech position of the U.S., right?" The PR man nods respectfully.

After promising to be back on time, Steve scoops me up. "Let's take a walk," he says, already out the door. His features make an impression—dark hair, dark eyes, and a prominent, pointy nose. Like an automobile aerodynamically designed to break the wind, Steve's profile seems made to slice through barriers.

"This is Apple," he announces, taking long strides as he leads the way to breakfast at his hangout, the Good Earth coffee shop. "We have twenty-six buildings within a ten-mile radius. We've done a very poor job of facilities planning. We're in the process of buying a few hundred acres right now. We want to build Apple campus—pull it all back together and build a college campus type environment."

Steve insists his skin doesn't tingle when he drives into the company parking lot each morning in his new Mercedes and surveys the empire he built from nothing. He's not Napoleon examining the map of Europe. "It's not like 'me' or 'mine,'" he corrects me with a certain edge to his voice when the possibility of ego is raised. "It's 'us' and 'ours.' There's a lot of fine people here. See, hardly anybody leaves. The cumulative turnover in the last five years has been under 10 percent. And most of that consists of people who have been working on the line. The way you can tell is by looking at the badge numbers of the most recently hired. We've got about 3800 employees and badge numbers are only up to about 4300."

Though Steve paints a glowing picture of a classless society, he is much more than just another employee. He owns badge #1 as well as far more stock in the company than anyone else, including co-founders Steve Wozniak, who left Apple to create the "US" music/technology festivals, but who now plans to return as Apple prepares to slug it out with IBM for control of the personal computer market, and Apple president, Mike Markkula, who plans to retire soon. On the day this interview was conducted, Steve's 7.5 million shares of Apple were worth approximately $427 million.

"My goal has always been to pass $1 billion a year in sales with under five thousand people, and we're going to do that this year, I think," Steve said. "And I'd like to pass $10 billion with under 10,000 employees. If we can do that and keep the number of people down, we can spend a lot of time with each person. And we can continue a company where the values don't get lost as they move down management."

Steve never specifically articulates what those values are, but he doesn't have to. When Republicans promised Americans a chicken in every pot and two cars in every garage, they didn't need to explain why either. Steve Jobs wants to put a personal computer in every home in America. You can't argue with universal prosperity.

Skirting a lawn sprinkler, he launches into an explanation of the effect of the "petrochemical revolution" on human society and then proceeds to describe the next revolution in human evolution, the "electronic revolution." "The computer is like an automobile, except you traverse conceptual space rather than physical space," he explains.

Steve's intelligence is intimidating. He can discuss anything from French cinema to how nutrition patterns are affected by the structure of the human jaw. "To take a very crude example, an Apple II uses less power than a thirty-watt light bulb, yet can generally save you an hour or two a day," he says. "In the future these things are going to be used as devices for people to express themselves, to turn the incredible amount of information they're getting into knowledge. I think we're going to see a restructuring of a lot of the ways people live, more important, the quality of their lives."

Steve was never Apple's premiere computer wizard, though he is a wizard nonetheless. It was Wozniak, with the assistance of Steve, Jerry Mannock and Rod Holt, who designed the Apple II, the computer that is the cornerstone of the company. But it was Jobs who understood its potential. His genius is in painting a vision of the future and leading others towards it. Wozniak was the first person he led.

"He has been able to make normal talented people perform superhuman feats," said a former Apple executive. "Steve has been able to do this with a handful of really talented engineers by trying every technique in the book to motivate them and get better effort out of them. He gets them to do things that are impossible; they start to believe, 'Hey, Steve knows I can do this video circuitry in eight integrated circuits instead of thirty-two. What the hell, I'll give it a try.' And he'll cajole them, browbeat them, play the spurned lover, make them feel guilty, and try every trick in the book to make them pull a rabbit out of a hat."

"The way we run Apple is by values," said Steve, returning to his theme. "You've heard of management by objective? We don't use that management system. Apple's the fastest-growing company in American corporate history, and when you're growing that fast the only thing you can do is hire incredibly great people and let them go to it. In general, we hire people who tell us what to do."

Steve may actually believe that and other statements such as, "I'm the street sweeper in the Mac Group. I end up doing most of the dog work." He is referring to the Macintosh, a powerful new personal computer that has been Steve's pet project for the past two years.

But his style is to take control. "He's pretty autocratic," the former executive noted. "A fairly typical interchange would go like this: While walking around, he would see something an engineer was working on and would say, 'Hey, what are you up to?' They'd start having a friendly chat about it, and Steve would decide there was something he didn't like about it. He would use very explicit language, critical language to describe how he felt.

"He was noted for walking through engineering and leaving a path of debris," the former associate continued. "It's well-intentioned. It's just that he has this incredibly strong desire to get the right answers. He has a strong respect for his intuition and the answers he arrives at."

"I get ticked. I'm a perfectionist. I like really good people," Steve explained. "I have a hard time settling for less than great work because I feel we are doing this for a lot of people out there. Any product we design now we're not going to do unless we can sell millions. There's millions of people out there, and they need great computers. So I'm hard on people sometimes. The people I work with everyday like it, I think. They wouldn't work anywhere else 'cause they end up doing better work than they thought they could."

The proof is in the pudding. Eight years ago Apple did not exist. In 1982, it rang up sales of $583 million ranking it 411th in sales on the Fortune 500, 201st in profit, and 26th in return on equity. Much of the credit for that explosive growth must go to Steve Jobs.

"On one level he's almost godlike in the kind of personal power he can wield with people," an Apple associate observed. "I'm not even talking about the fact that he's a rich guy who runs a successful company. Just simple personal power. And that's what really turns a lot of people on. There's a real sense of being close to a very powerful energy source."

The owner of the Good Earth coffee shop waves to Steve as he walks in the door. "When we left the garage after a year," he says, referring to his parent's garage in Los Gatos, legendary now, where he and "Woz" assembled the first Apples, "we got an office in a building right back here and we had one thousand square feet. We were trembling because we didn't have the money to pay the rent for more than three months. We rapidly ran out of space, so this became our conference room. We used to have orange juice conferences here around eleven in the morning. They gave me a little plaque one time as their most popular customer."

Steve sits down and orders a glass of orange juice. His eccentricities—his vegetarianism, casual dress code, and drug experiences—have become the stuff of myth. While essentially accurate, they seem less important to Steve than to the media. In the early days of Apple, those personality quirks were exploited by Regis McKenna, Silicon Valley's premiere PR man, who created the image of a hippie David competing against the pin-striped Goliaths at IBM and Texas Instruments. Though Steve still cherishes his counterculture credentials, he has shaved off his beard and cut his hair. He takes seriously his status as the crown prince of American capitalism.

He was despondent for several weeks after he addressed a magazine publishers convention in Puerto Rico where he was introduced as a hippie with hundred dollar bills falling out of his pockets. "I was really ticked and I got up and talked about that," he said. "I told them it was very frustrating to grow and change and not have people recognize it."

Still, one can't help but cling to the fairytale of Apple's origins. It's a wonderful story and Steve loves telling it. "We didn't intend to go into business," he begins. "The reason we built this thing is because we wanted a computer for ourselves."

They made their computer from parts that Steve "liberated" from his job at Atari and that Wozniak got from Hewlett-Packard where he was working at the time. When their friends saw the machine, they all wanted one too. To satisfy demand but not spend every waking hour assembling computers, they paid a friend $1,300 to do the artwork for a printed circuit board that cut assembly time from sixty hours to six. To raise the $1,300, Steve sold his Volkswagen bus and Woz his Hewlett-Packard 65 calculator.

"You could just plug in the parts to this thing and solder it, and it would work," said Steve, still sounding amazed that it did. "So what we were going to do was sell blank circuit boards to our friends and hope to sell maybe one hundred of them. We could make them for $25. We figured if we could sell them for $50, we could make $2,500 profit and recoup our transportation costs and calculation abilities."

Since they didn't have the money to make the boards they decided it would be prudent to collect cash up front. "So I was out trying to sell some of these boards one day, and the Byte Shop, this computer store down in El Camino, said, 'I'll take fifty.'"

Visions of computer assembly lines danced in Steve's head. "Of course we saw dollar signs," he admitted. "The only hitch is that the Byte Shop wanted the machines fully assembled." That required thousands of dollars worth of parts. So Steve went out and he did what he does better than anyone else. He convinced people to buy into his dream. "I went down to three local electronics parts distributors and on sheer enthusiasm convinced them to sell us about $25,000 worth of parts on thirty-days credit. We had no assets. Just nothing. And they took a gamble.

"So we built one hundred computers. We delivered fifty to the Byte Shop for cash, took the cash over and paid the distributors in twenty-nine days. We run the business on cash flow to this day."

As a child of the television age, Steve didn't have to be explained the importance of advertising. He asked Regis McKenna to represent him. "I figured as long as we couldn't afford anybody, we might as well not afford the best," he recalled. McKenna turned Steve down three times. That only whetted his appetite. "Finally, the fourth time I said, 'Regis, I have no money to pay you. I want you to do our ads. We're going to be an incredibly successful computer company. Trust me. Just trust me. I'll pay you in a year. And he looked me right in the eye and he said, 'Okay.'"

Steve exhibits the same tenacity in his personal as in his professional life. One story involves a beautiful woman he met on a flight from Munich to Paris with whom he instantly fell in love. He saw her at the airport check-in line but got separated from her—one of the drawbacks of flying first class when your peers travel tourist. When the plane landed he located her at the baggage claim and started to chat with her. They shared a cab into Paris and made a tentative date to meet for dinner. Steve fell asleep when he arrived at his hotel and awoke twenty minutes late for the appointment. He rushed out the door and through pouring rain to the bridge overlooking the Seine where they had arranged to meet. She wasn't there and he'd forgotten to get her address or phone number.

"He turned the world upside down looking for her," Regis McKenna recalled. "He got somebody in the French government to look up the passport. He really searched."

Steve did finally locate her. She was a well-known model, and she was living with a man in New York. Steve said he never contacted her.

In any event, Jobs is a true romantic. "I was in an executive staff meeting with all the officers in the company, and Steve turns to me and says, 'Can I talk to you for a minute?' recalled Trip Hawkins, a former Apple executive the same age as Steve, who left Apple to start his own company. "So we go sit in his office. At the time I was going out with a woman six years older than me who had children. Steve started to ask me all these questions about what it's like. And then he starts telling me he's going out with a woman who's older and has some kids. We talk about it for forty-five minutes. It was a delightful conversation; it wasn't until about four months later that I figured out he was talking about Joan Baez."

Steve's personality seems to be less warm than it is compelling in its self-absorption. He doesn't share confidences; he bestows them. He draws you into his dream. "Almost on the spur of the moment, he can have a conversation with you and tell you things that make you feel as if you're having great secrets revealed to you," Trip Hawkins said.

His ego is epic. According to Apple insiders, Steve started the Macintosh project after Vice-President John Couch was given management responsibility for developing "Lisa," Apple's powerful new office computer. Steve recruited some of Apple's best engineers, sequestered them at a separate facility, and had them work in direct competition with "Lisa." At one point Steve and Couch had a $5000 bet about which product would hit the marketplace first.

Steve insists ego played no part in the Macintosh project. "I felt the Lisa project was getting a little too large," he said. "I felt Apple needed another small personal computer." He confirmed the existence of the $5000 bet, but said its purpose was to get the people working on both projects "fired up."

Steve's standards for people are so high few can measure up to them—even though he seems to be on a continuous quest for those who can. Hiring John Sculley from Pepsico, where he was their whiz-kid president, to take over the presidency of Apple was an act of bravado and brilliance that may prove as important to Steve's personal development as to Apple's. "Talking with him is amazing," a satisfied Steve told a reporter for Apple's in-house newspaper. "When you explain something to him, his comprehension is far beyond what you've told him."

"No one tells Steve he's an ass anymore—which I think is what people need to tell him," an industry analyst said. "I suspect Sculley is, and that's why Steve is crazy about Sculley from everything I can see."

Steve's father is a machinist who fixes cars for fun. "I have a real simple family and they have real simple values, but they're strong on them," Steve said.

"They're very simple people," said Regis McKenna, picking up on Steve's description. McKenna has never met them, although Steve is as close to Regis as to anyone and often spends evenings and weekends with him and his family. "They're just very good, hardworking people who, more than anything else, allowed his personality to flourish. They're not real visible in the kind of world he's in."

Steve is adopted, and after dropping out of Reed College in Oregon after one semester, experimenting with LSD, and traveling to India, he embarked on a search for his real parents. One associate attributes his monumental drive to that quest. "My own Freudian point of view is that he's trying to get so much attention that he can be on a pedestal so that high above the rest of the landscape his real parents will recognize him and realize the error of their ways."

Steve rejects the theory. "This is really stupid. It's just not true," he said. "My monumental drive has nothing to do with that. I really believe the reason I'm trying to do what I do is because I actually love doing it."

Steve claims to be unaffected by his wealth. "You've got to remember this happened pretty slowly," he said. When you're twenty-eight and working in an industry where strategic advantage is measured in microseconds, eight years is a long time. "We went public in September 1980. People said, 'God, you've got all this money. It's going to change you.' My response was, 'I was worth a million dollars on paper when I was twenty-three, ten million when I was twenty-four, and a hundred million when I was twenty-five. I had several years to figure out what I thought about all this stuff before it got to epidemic proportions."

But others find Steve's attitude toward money ambivalent. "On the one hand he'll tell you things like, 'I don't feel like it's my money. I'm just its keeper for a few decades.' On the other hand, he's the kind of guy the price of Apple stock is very important to. He's got a lot of pride tied up in his net worth," Trip Hawkins said. Since Apple went public, Steve has sold virtually none of his shares.

When the price of Apple stock plummeted recently, reflecting the overall competitiveness of the personal computer industry, the *Wall Street Journal* reported Steve's net worth dropped $278 million. Steve claims to be unperturbed by this turn of events. "I never worry about the stock price," he asserts. "I worry about running the business. The stock price will reflect how well we run Apple.

"In another year to eighteen months there will be only two companies that emerge from the smoke," he added. "Those companies will be Apple and IBM. And I believe Apple will emerge very strong."

Steve lives like both the prince and the pauper. His Tudor-style house in California is sparsely furnished though he moved in several years ago. Yet, he also bought a duplex apartment overlooking Central Park in Manhattan and hired I.M. Pei to design it.

Ultimately, it's power more than money that intrigues Steve. Since he's on the leading edge of technology, he's got loads of it. He's met with the president of France, leaders of Congress, and anyone who counts at the White House.

"Apple has a social responsibility to share some of the things we think about what the technology is going to be in five or ten years," Steve said. "My attitude is, if they want to know anything, we'll try to help them."

Last year Steve went to Washington to personally lobby 130 Congressmen and almost half the Senate to support a bill that would have allowed computer companies tax credits for donating computers to schools. The bill died in the Senate, but a similar bill passed in California. Under a program called "Kids Can't Wait," Apple is donating over nine thousand personal computers, one to virtually every elementary and secondary school in the state.

Steve has also started to speak out on the arms race and has raised eyebrows with his Strangelovian alternatives to nuclear deterrence. "Nuclear deterrence is a strategy that's fundamentally warped," he stated flatly. "So what you do is you let the Soviet Union build a beautiful bunker in Central Park, a real nice one with statues and waterfalls and a hundred megaton hydrogen device below. And we do the same under their cities, and it's all over. Mutually guaranteed annihilation. We don't need to spend another dime. Just minor maintenance."

He added that he only espouses the theory because it underlines the absurdity of the arms race. "The concept of nuclear war is Strangelovian, so the minute you start talking about it you sound Strangelovian," he said. "I am actually a proponent of unilateral disarmament. But I think that would never fly in this country."

Whatever his political dreams for the future, at the moment Steve seems committed to Apple. Spectacular as his success has been, he believes it's only the overture to what he and his Apple corps is capable of accomplishing. He refers to the last eight years as "bootcamp."

"We've done a good job, but we have a chance to do a great job in the next five years if we can really pull it off," he said. "I was on my way to Japan to sit in a monastery when all this started, so I sort of consider this monastery experience."

Lisa
Birnbach

Photo by Lawrence Robins

Sherry Lansing and Mary Cunningham met through a mutual friend. That friend was twenty-five-year-old Lisa Birnbach, who wrote cover stories on both women for *Parade* magazine. It was the first time Lansing gave an extensive interview since becoming president of 20th Century Fox and the first time Cunningham granted an interview since resigning as vice-president of the Bendix Corporation amid rumors she was romantically involved with boss Bill Agee.

Lisa's gift is to make friends wherever she goes, and her interviews with both women quickly led to friendships. When Mary married Bill Agee, she invited Lisa to her wedding reception and had lunch with her the next day. She calls her frequently and has even sent Lisa copies of speeches she has written.

Sherry Lansing agreed to the *Parade* story because she was impressed with the way Lisa handled the Cunningham piece. It sounded less like an exposé than an exchange of confidences. Lisa interviewed Sherry in Los Angeles and New York and in the first-class cabins of planes jetting between the two cities. They got along so well that, at one point, Lisa worried her friendship with Sherry might hinder her ability to write about America's first female movie mogul.

"Sherry was fascinated by Mary," Lisa said. "She felt real sympathy for Mary."

Lisa arranged for the women to meet in Mary's Park Avenue office where she worked as an executive with Joseph E. Seagram & Son, Inc. They were very different: Mary was extremely reserved and Sherry was effusive. But they had something in common in their admiration for Lisa. They were discussing the future of the country and who its leaders would be, and Mary Cunningham pointed at her young writer friend.

If you've heard of Lisa Birnbach before it's probably as editor of *The Official Preppy Handbook.* She's the "Princess of Prep," the woman who transformed a stuffy style of behavior into a national craze. Her book was number one on the *New York Times* Best Seller list for twenty-two weeks.

But if you believe her editors, agents, and friends, *Preppy* is but the beginning of a brilliant career. Years from now they expect the book to be best remembered as a stepladder to the stars for one of the time's brightest young minds.

"It quickly became apparent to me that she wasn't some lucky, spoiled rich kid who happened to write a book," said Walter Anderson, the editor of *Parade* magazine, of his first meeting with Lisa. "Her humor was the result of a deep and abiding intellect and extraordinary curiosity. I just knew she had great desire and I said to her, 'Well Lisa, ten years from now are you still going to be the preppy queen?'

"I listened to her closely, how she articulated, and her passions, and then I realized what I had in front of me. I realized, given the opportunity, this young woman would achieve just about anything she wanted." Lisa was recently made a contributing editor to *Parade*. "I have every reason to believe forty or fifty years from now when I'm retired and sitting by the edge of some lake, I can think back and say, 'I remember when.'"

In jeans and a grey sweatshirt (yes, she's wearing a frayed yellow alligator shirt underneath it), Lisa Birnbach doesn't look like a leader of nations. She recently moved into an airy apartment overlooking Greenwich Village, but what with writing a screenplay for Paramount, *Lisa Birnbach's College Guide* for Villard Books/Ballantine, articles for *Parade*, and performing *The Official Preppy Comedy Hour* at dozens of colleges, she hasn't had time to unpack. Stranded on a sofa chair in a sea of boxes filled with junk dating back to nursery school, Lisa looks like a freshman moving into her dorm on the first day of the fall semester.

"I felt very proprietary about preppies," said Lisa, explaining why she gave up her job as a staff writer at the *Village Voice* to edit and help write a book which guaranteed her only twelve weeks salary and a small percentage of the profits. "Preppiness was the glue that bonded my friends and me together at Brown University. Some people had drug humor; others had Jewish humor. This was our shared sensibility. We really sat around and talked about what is a preppy? What's a preppy disease? I even had a preppy party my junior year.

"In the end I didn't know if it would sell, and I didn't know what I'd do afterwards, but I just couldn't let anyone else do the book."

On a Saturday in May, 1980, Lisa assembled the best minds in prepdom—bankers, jocks, stockbrokers, debutantes—at her parents' Park Avenue apartment to brainstorm the book. It was scheduled to be published in the fall.

"She just has this ability to come off the wall with very creative ideas," said Bill Lichtenstein, who was one of Lisa's classmates at Brown. "She can inspire people to pick up on her energy and her creativity and to move with it."

Bookstores showed only moderate interest in the *Handbook* before it was published, but once they got hold of the finished product and saw that it wasn't just another joke book but an upbeat little bible about a segment of American society, (and one with purchasing power), they deluged Workman Publishing with orders. A national publicity tour was arranged, and Lisa was hastily dispatched to spread the gospel according to Preppies.

Suddenly, in her Top-Siders, knee socks, kilt, down vest thrown over an alligator shirt, and pearls, Lisa was everywhere you looked. She loved the limelight, and she had the wit, the coed sparkle, and the natural timing to charm everyone from college kids to grandmothers.

The city of Charlottesville, home of the University of Virginia, declared November 19, 1980, "Official Preppy Day" and treated Lisa like a homecoming queen. When Lisa asked students at Southern Methodist University in Texas how many of them owned BMWs and Mercedes, they answered by throwing their car keys onto the stage. She appeared on the "Today" show three times in one year, probably some sort of record for anyone other than a head of state.

It wasn't unusual for Lisa to return to her hotel room exhausted after a round of TV and radio interviews only to find a crowd of people waiting for her in the lobby wanting to buy her a drink or take her along to a party. "I think one of the reasons I did so well was because the book was well-timed and well-written. I hate to talk this way about myself," she said, her voice rising self-consciously, "but I think I'm likable out there. I think people think I'm down-to-earth and unassuming.

"I don't want to make myself out to be this modest, unwitting person who doesn't care about fame," she added. "I love to be recognized."

Lisa so saturated the airwaves that only months after she hit the road, stewardesses on planes would greet her with, "I suppose Miss Preppie will want a seat in the smoking section?"

"Once I was at this pharmacy," Lisa recalled. "I was holding a box of, ah, feminine hygiene equipment and someone came up to me and said, 'Miss Birnbach?' and I was like," Lisa pantomimes juggling the box behind her back trying to make it vanish, "I don't want them to see these. I don't have to have a mentrual cycle. I've been on Merv Griffin."

As soon as they saw her on TV, college lecture agents realized Lisa's money-making potential. Kevin Flaherty, Lisa's lecture agent, booked a national college tour for her before he'd ever spoken with her. At first Lisa balked at the idea of speaking in front of hundreds of people, but eventually the ham in her took control. Today she commands $4000 a show and has performed *The Official Preppy Comedy Hour* at close to a hundred colleges. "It was a lengendary tour that spring," Flaherty recalled. "The word of mouth was incredible. People called her the funniest woman alive. She became a kind of hero. Some people identified with, 'Wow, she's our age and she's had this incredible success.' But more than anything else it was, 'She's very funny.'"

When Lisa was an ugly adolescent her parents told her she'd be pretty one day. When she was struggling with math in grammar school, they told her she was smart anyway. They have stood by her throughout the preppy odyssey. In September of 1982, after the *Handbook* sold a million copies, Lisa's parents celebrated by renting a mansion, inviting two hundred of Lisa's friends to lunch, and bringing the Whiffenpoofs down from Yale to serenade her. The Preppy Seal—a duck paddling past crossed tennis racquets and a croquet mallet surrounded by the inscription "Semper Preparatus" (forever Prep)—shone over the party like the sun over a fairy-tale kingdom.

Kim Rubin, Lisa's best friend from high school, believes Lisa's instincts as a performer come from her mother. "Lisa's mom talks a lot," said Kim, who is now a lawyer in Boston. Lisa said that neither she, her father, nor her two younger brothers are sure what her mother does, but that she's always pleasant and occupied. Lisa's father is a successful gem importer. One of Lisa's brothers is a junior at Union College, and the other one, who is exactly two years younger than Lisa, is a fledgling executive at an advertising agency.

In short, the Birnbachs are a fairly typical wealthy family, and Lisa had a fairly typical wealthy upbringing. She wore braces, attended all-girls schools, and mostly just dreamed of boys. They didn't dream about her. Her gangly, five-foot-ten frame was not the stuff of adolescent male fantasies. "I'm telling you, I was no prize," said Lisa. "I really did feel very homely. I was also very unpopular for a long time."

Mysteriously, she always remained an optimist. Lisa recalls that moment of truth when she received her S.A.T. scores. "I was so delighted," she said. "I was jumping up and down shouting, 'I got a 520! I got a 520 in math!' Until I realized my whole class got 780s. I knew I was smart, even when I got a 520, but I worried that I'd be hostage to my S.A.T. scores, that I could only date guys who would go out with girls who had 520s."

Lisa needn't have worried. After spending her freshman year at Barnard College, she transferred to Brown where she paraded, or rather stampeded onto the social scene. "In college I was an entertainer from the beginning," she recalled. "That was out of nervousness too. My first year at Brown, I didn't eat more than one course at the same table in the dining hall. When I think back on it, I was so frantic it was terrible. I probably seemed superficial to some people."

Mercifully, the doctors had "surgically removed" the glasses Lisa had worn throughout high school and replaced them with contact lenses, revealing eyes that were warm and full of mirth. "I had a boyfriend my second day," said Lisa not so much with pride as with relief. "I had male friends for the first time. I loved the idea that guys liked my company. I always have felt, and this is really sexist and unfair, that men are funnier than women."

The protagonist of the movie Lisa's writing for Paramount is a male. "It's set in 1977 and it's about college students having to finally make the break and leave school. I'm using the same anxiety I had, but in a guy."

Guys liked Lisa as much as she liked them. "If you look at her objectively, she's pretty, but she's not excessively attractive," said a classmate of Lisa's from Brown. "But there would always be guys chasing her all over the place. As soon as they saw her, guys would fall in love with her."

Lisa has definite personal magnetism. She wants people to like her, so she performs for them. Yet her supreme talent is not that she's a good talker, but rather an even better listener; not that she's extremely witty but rather that she makes people she meets believe they're just as witty as she is.

She remembers names and faces better than most professional politicians. After spending a day at Hofstra University on Long Island researching her *College Book* and spending the evening performing for several hundred students there, she bid farewell to more than a dozen students she'd met, remembering each of their names and something important about them. Simply stated, Lisa makes other people feel as if they count.

On the *Today* show when host Tom Brokaw joked, "Lisa doesn't really take this so seriously, although she does take the money seriously," Lisa replied, "Tom, how vulgar. I would never ask you how much you made." A friend who has worked with Lisa for several years believes *Preppy* has made her a millionaire, but Lisa refuses to discuss the subject. She grew up with money and there are no signs her success has altered her life-style, except that she travels less frequently on the subway. There is nothing ostentatious about her. With some embarrassment, she admitted she'd bought a pair of Susan Bennis/Warren Edwards shoes, which start at $300. Later it slipped out she actually owned three pair. She bought Donna Gould, the director of publicity at Workman during the preppy years, a Rolex watch as a way of saying thanks for holding Lisa's hand over the telephone while she moved from hotel room to hotel room during the *Preppy* book tour.

The most important thing money has bought Lisa is freedom. "*Preppy* has given me so much exposure that I can choose my projects right now. And if these current projects work out fairly well, I think I can depart from anything commercial and try to do something else if I'm ready."

Strip away the one-liners that Lisa tosses off the way a vending machine dispenses Mars Bars, and she is serious, forever sober. "People at college thought I was stoned or tripping because of the way I behaved," she said. "They said, 'Wouldn't it be great to see Lisa on acid!' Or they'd say, 'You'd love her, she's crazy.' I'm not crazy at all. I'm one of the most conservative people I know. But wearing a funny hat to dinner or doing a Charo imitation made me 'crazy.'"

In college, Lisa may not have had the self-confidence to correct people who thought she was nothing more than a lovable clown, but that's no longer the case. During question-and-answer sessions with college students after the *Preppy Comedy Hour*, she always manages to mention her support for gun-control legislation. And when she spoke at Duke University at the time they were considering building a library for former President Richard Nixon's official papers, Lisa spoke out forcefully against it.

"I realized what a lucky position I was in compared to Gordon Liddy or Abby Hoffman or Timothy Leary. I'm not only the youngest person on the lecture circuit; I'm accessible to these people. I really have their ear," she said.

It was based on Lisa's college following that *Rolling Stone* magazine asked her to write the cover story for their first college supplement. Entitled "Scared Serious," it blasted campus apathy. If people expect *Lisa Birnbach's College Book* to be a look at the lighter side of college life, they're in for a shock. "Students now are profoundly different from when I went to college," said Lisa sounding middle-aged. "Today's students are not fighting the federal cutbacks in financial aid. They're voting for Reagan. They're proudly showing me their Young Republican offices. They're all business majors, and they're concerned about making money."

Lisa is no bomb-thrower herself, but she does occasionally have anarchistic impulses. She wore a whistle when she worked as an ad agency trainee in the "traffic" division on her first job out of college. "Traffic" coordinates the multitude of agency operations and Lisa didn't hesitate to blow her whistle whenever oversized egos jammed at busy intersections.

The last thing the real Lisa wants to be identified as is a preppy. "Part of me doesn't like to be detected. I don't like to be pegged," she said. "People college age and younger take this preppy stuff very seriously, and I'm there to say, 'Yuk, yuk, yuk, I don't take myself seriously doing this and neither should you.'"

Lisa, who is Jewish, thinks the reason the *Preppy Handbook* works so well is because it was written from the perspective of an outsider. "Could a WASP have written the *Preppy Handbook*?" she asked. "I think the book works because of the knowledge of the inside with the perspective of the outside. If it had been written in a more serious tone of voice, it would have been elitist, it would have been snotty, it would have been a turnoff. If it had been written any sillier, it would have looked uninformed. So it's that straddling of being Jewish."

Though Lisa is a performer and often works in collaboration with others there is something solitary and driven about her. On Halloween night she didn't attend any crazy costume party, but instead sat alone in a hotel room near the University of Wisconsin and wrote her Sherry Lansing story. After spending a month on the road, she's capable of coming home, locking herself in her apartment for a full weekend, living on take-out Chinese food, and working. "One of my secrets is that I really am a hard worker," she admitted. "I try to disguise that fact from a lot of people. I guess that's because I wanted to be a party girl. Part of me always wanted to be popular."

"Think of it," said Maureen Salter, who worked in Publicity at Workman and now works full time for Lisa. "You're twenty-three years old, getting up at five o'clock in the morning, flying on planes that are so small they weigh you, and you're doing this for months at a time. You have to give up years of your life, relationships, friendships. A lot of people get jealous because they only see the publicity. They see the fun and they see the glamour, but they don't see you get two hours of sleep. They don't see you cry on the phone because you're so tired; and then you have to go meet some interviewer who asks you, 'Isn't it fun making a lot of money?'"

People did get jealous. Some of the same people who had happily thrown around ideas at Lisa's parents' apartment accused Lisa, in magazines like *New York* and *Newsweek*, of grabbing all the glory on a collaborative effort. In fact, Lisa shared writer credit with Jonathan Roberts, who brought the idea for a preppy spoof to Workman in the first place, Carol Wallace, and Mason Wiley. A few other writers contributed a paragraph here and there, but their contributions were not credited by name, and they received little money and recognition. Only Lisa and Jonathan Roberts shared in a small percentage of the book profits. All four of them shared in the subsidiary profits. Lisa said that she is not to blame, because contributors worked out their own deals with publisher Peter Workman, and she insisted, "I never called it 'my book' on tour. I can't stress that enough. It was 'our book' or 'the book.' And I was never 'the author.' I was 'the editor.'"

"Lisa may not have written that whole book, but she totally publicized it," said Donna Gould in her defense. "Without Lisa, *Preppy* would never have made it. There are a lot of sore losers in the game. It's called jealousy."

"That was really an upsetting time in my life," Lisa recalled. "I was on tour when the articles came out. I was being interviewed on the noon news somewhere, and I got a call from Workman saying there was going to be this article and people were talking about this and that. I hated to start interviews with, 'How's your lawsuit going?' There was no lawsuit."

Despite her enormous talent for making friends, Lisa never became friends with her publisher. Lisa said she had a personality conflict with Peter Workman. "There was a lot of resentment there towards me, because they felt I was getting too big for my britches. What they didn't like was that Lisa Birnbach was getting equal billing to the *Preppy Handbook*. People were as interested in me as in the book."

When asked if she has any hints for success, Lisa replies, "Find an agent you can trust." That doesn't sound like very helpful advice for someone on the outside trying to get a foot in the door, but after the battering Lisa's reputation took, it has become an obsession with her. She has surrounded herself with a team of agents, lawyers, accountants, and friends whom she trusts implicitly. "She knows who her friends are and who her friends are not," said Donna Gould.

Maureen, Lisa's assistant, behaves like a sister, reminding Lisa that she's late for lunch or that she's forgotten her wallet again. And Esther Newberg, Lisa's superagent at I.C.M., treats Lisa as if she were a prize filly on her way to the third leg of the Triple Crown. "I see her as a major writer," stated Newberg. "And she has a career as a screenwriter ahead of her also."

Still, Lisa is by no means a pushover. She can issue instructions to Maureen with the sureness of a president of a

Fortune 500 corporation, and she's not afraid to disagree
with anyone. "I have a big enough ego that I'm not totally
motivated by niceness," she said. "I think I'm interesting,
and if other people miss that, that's their loss."

Within two weeks after she signed with I.C.M., Lisa had
signed her movie contract with Paramount and her book
contract with Villard Books/Ballantine. Her agents take Lisa
to those Hollywood parties the rest of us just read about.
They're grooming their client for a place in the pantheon of
popular culture.

At one such party, Lisa mingled with the likes of Shelley
Duvall, Penny Marshall, Teri Garr, and Michael O'Don-
oghue, the creator of "Saturday Night Live." "I have this re-
tarded star-struck thing," said Lisa. "I felt like going over to
every single person there and saying, 'I love your work.' I felt
like a fan."

The stars don't treat Lisa like a fan. After Lisa appeared
on *Real People,* Sara Purcell, the show's host, called Lisa.
"Why is she calling me?" Lisa asked herself. "Does she call
the mud wrestlers she interviews too?" Purcell wanted to
establish a friendship and they've since become friends.

"In Los Angeles, people I don't even know will say, 'Why
don't you stay here next time you come out,' or, 'Let me give
you a party.' There's a kind of instant friendship that you
have out there. Who knows how real it is. Who knows how
long lasting it'll be. In New York, if I met someone who was
visiting from out of town, I would not immediately offer
them a party or a place to stay. I mean immediately, even
before they know you. Again, if I weren't Lisa Birnbach with
the *Preppy Handbook* after my name, I don't know if those
invitations would be offered."

Lisa's greatest professional challenge is to make people
drop the *Preppy Handbook* after her name. The only way
she'll succeed is by producing a work on her own of the
highest quality. "Before the *Preppy Handbook* did so well, I
was probably headed in one direction—writing. Now there
are goals all over the place which is great. But it means I
don't know where I'll be pegged when I'm eighty. My fervent
hope is that when I am eighty, I'm not still referred to as 'the
Preppy Handbook author.'"

According to Lisa, she hasn't changed much since that

time she met Paul Newman at the age of seventeen. "I was wearing this T-shirt that said, Je Suis American. We shook hands, and because I was in a state of stupefaction and wouldn't let go of his hand, somebody felt they had to say something, so he said, 'Je Suis American,' with a very strong French accent."

Lisa would rather forget her dazed, teenybopper reply. "I laughed my head off, and I said, 'I didn't think anyone would notice.'"

She claims she wouldn't react any differently today. "I'd probably swoon. I think I'd still be rendered speechless," she said.

"Well," she added, adjusting slightly for her success, "Maybe I'd say, 'Let's have lunch.'"

Chip Fichtner

Chip Fichtner *is not driving the Rolls tonight, or the* Model T Ford roadster, or the 1959 candy red Cadillac convertible with the giant tailfins, or the pickup truck. He's driving the Porsche 928, too fast, through downtown Dallas while dialing a number on the car's telephone. "Hi," he says softly to the person who answers, as if he were speaking from his bedroom. "What's up?"

What's up is that, at age twenty-three, Charles "Chip" Fichtner, who is running his own multimillion dollar commodities brokerage firm, a telex time-sharing company, and a housing development company, is buying up every available piece of real estate in historic East Dallas and trying to juggle a demanding social schedule.

"There's no one else out at the ranch," he lies. "I swear I'm going to sit in the hot tub for five minutes, and then I'm going to bed. I'm totally exhausted."

He hands the phone to a male passenger to convince his friend there isn't some blond bombshell sitting next to him, takes the phone back to make suggestive promises, and finally gets off. These are the kinds of complications that make sane men mad but keep Chip Fichtner sane.

"Chip does not limit the parameters of his potential growth," explained a broker at Chip's commodity company, Contemporary Financial Corporation. "I've never seen a more perfect example of someone whose imagination and belief in himself is limitless."

Another way of putting it is that Chip left his home state, Connecticut, because the state wasn't big enough to contain his ego. It just about fits in Texas. "It's the land of opportunity," he said pulling into the parking lot of a bar which caters to the legions of young professionals who live in the surrounding singles complexes. "Dallas is a town based on ability instead of experience. You're not going to be president of a bank in New York before you're thirty. Down here I can name five bank presidents under thirty. They like to see young people succeed here. It reflects well on the town."

Chances are Chip would have succeeded even if he'd stayed back east. He's been making money since he was twelve when he bought up all the paper routes in his Greenwich, Connecticut, neighborhood. One can often ascribe an individual's drive to an overbearing parent or environmental factors such as poverty. But in Chip's case the secret of his success seems to be hidden in his chromosomes.

"Even as a very small infant he was not very cuddly," remembered Chip's father. "You'd pick him up, and he'd be happy to be held for thirty seconds. Then he was wiggling and squirming and ready to get down and go and do something on his own. When he left grade school his teacher told us he was twelve going on twenty-one. He knew Chip would never have a problem succeeding in the world."

If there's a method to Chip's success, it might best be described by the commodity brokers' term "contrary opinion."

Loosely translated it means going against the crowd. "Your average American investor will read the newspaper and if it says, 'Housing starts in Dallas are at a record high,' he'll think, 'Wow, I'll buy lumber!' said Chip, sitting in his office spitting tobacco juice into a brass spittoon between sentences. "The problem is that John Doe who just read the newspaper is about six weeks behind what's happening. The people who bought the lumber six weeks ago bought it on the theory that housing starts haven't gone up yet but they think they will because interest rates are going down, the economy is getting better, it's springtime, the average income of people has gone up, and the tax rates have gone down. They're 'in,' in advance.

"I did a radio show when silver was $40," Chip continues with characteristic exuberance. "The show was a debate between me and this broker from Smith Barney. The Smith Barney guy said, 'Gold and silver is going up. Everybody is buying. I'm getting calls every fifteen minutes from janitors, doctors, everybody wants to buy silver.'

"My rebuttal was, 'This is probably the greatest time in my life I've seen to *sell* silver, and I've been a silver bull for two years. If you're smart you'll dump every piece of silver you own, because when the average citizen is getting in, the price is going to go down.'" Within weeks of Chip's prophecy the price of silver plummeted.

Still, it's not as simple as Chip makes it sound. "Chip is a very, very smart person," said Grant Curtis, Chip's best friend from high school and a fellow commodities professional. "When it comes to books, Chip is a wizard. Chip will read something and get twice as much out of it as somebody else."

In addition to the Dallas papers, Chip reads the *New York Times* and the *Wall Street Journal* each morning and also subscribes to thirty periodicals a month. "He has a tremendous mind for seeing opportunities, and the courage and belief in himself to act on it," a business associate said. "He can see more than just what is on the surface. He can listen to an offhand comment and zero in on it. He will opportunize on things that other people don't even realize exist."

An example of that occurred during a casual conversation between Chip and Jethro Pugh, the former defensive tackle for the Dallas Cowboys football team and Chip's neighbor. Jethro was describing his work: He's an independent insurance adjuster, which means he represents the claimant in negotiations with the insurance company over settlements. In an offhand way, Chip inquired whether Jethro worked for himself. When he said he worked for someone else, Chip spontaneously said, "Let's incorporate." He immediately set up a meeting between Jethro and a local hotshot public relations man. Chip was convinced that Jethro's illustrious football career, combined with his current consumer expertise, would land him on every talk show in America and launch Jethro Pugh independent insurance adjuster offices coast to coast.

Chip has had this ability forever. As a twelve-year-old, he employed fifteen kids in a local lawn-care service, which grossed $18,000 in a single summer and gave Chip the cash to buy a cabin cruiser. He bought and sold sixty cars, trucks, fire engines, ambulances, and hearses before he was old enough to drive. During his senior year in high school he and a partner started Ticket Magic, a Broadway show ticket agency for Connecticut suburbanites who didn't want to make the trip into Manhattan to buy theatre tickets. It grossed $200,000 in ten months.

It was through silver that Chip got hooked on commodities. He was a freshman at Southern Methodist University in 1978 when he got a tip from the man who had advised the Hunt brothers to buy silver. Chip was broke after paying his tuition, but he somehow managed to borrow $5,000 from a local bank. He bought futures contracts for 10,000 ounces of silver. The price soared and earned him a six figure profit.

He quickly lost it all in more trading, but having stood at the high-stakes table with the heavy rollers, he wasn't much interested in freshman mixers anymore. Chip stayed in school just long enough to resurrect a fraternity that had been closed by the school administration because of its "Animal House" reputation. He became its president as a freshman, then dropped out to take a job as a flunky with a local brokerage firm.

While working there he observed that most brokers spent half their time trading their accounts into the ground, since commissions were made on volume rather than profitability, and the other half trying to drum up new clients after the old ones were killed off. Chip sensed a certain lack of logic to this process.

He focused on the idea of "managed commodity accounts." He wouldn't trade them himself, but would travel around the country to find the traders with the best track records in specific commodities and then team them up with clients. Chip took the idea to Merrill Lynch where his all-star team of traders made money for his clients at a time when other brokers were losing their shirts.

Chip made few friends pointing out his success and other's failures. "I was really obnoxious and brash," he said as if these were qualities that qualified one for sainthood. He almost got fired from Merrill Lynch for sending out an update on company letterhead with arrows in colored crayon pointing to his gains. "I was saying, 'Look, our performance has been dynamite. Get off your duff and send me more capital.' That particular piece of paper brought in $1.5 million worth of accounts."

Chip was moving too fast to maneuver his way through the corporate maze, and he let his superiors know it. "Heck, I was twenty years old, and here I was the biggest managed account guy in the country," he said.

According to Chip the brokerage firm of Bear, Stearns offered him a six-figure salary to head up their managed account department. At the age of twenty-one he was the youngest vice-president in the fifty-eight-year history of the company. But when the economy went into a nose dive in 1981, investors turned to more stable investments than commodities. "So I started taking it easy and screwing around with other entrepreneurial deals," said Chip who never took it easy a day in his life. "I kept the accounts I had and lived off the income which was okay."

Chip also occupied himself feeding his ego, playing the whiz kid being interviewed by *People* magazine and all the Dallas papers, and having lunch with Dallas big shots.

But Bear, Stearns was bearish on all the whiz-kid stuff, and Chip spent as much time in the general partner's office smoothing ruffled feathers as he did finding new clients. In 1982, Chip left the company and went into business on his own.

"Managed commodity accounts are on the rebound," said

Chip, holding up a check for $100,000 that had just arrived from a new investor. "Right now my personal income is more than double what it was last year working at Bear, Stearns." Chip hopes to gross close to three-quarters of a million dollars this year.

Chip attracts clients through eye-catching ads like the one in the *Wall Street Journal* which beckoned "Losers in Commodities?" He personally phones commodity losers and convinces them to be born again. "People said I was crazy," explained Chip, jettisoning tobacco juice. "They said, 'Don't go after the guy who's been killed. He's so burned out, he doesn't want to hear the word commodity ever again.' I said, 'That's not true. The guy got into commodities in the first place because he was willing to take the risk. He saw there was money to be made. He had money. He still has money. He's still willing to take the risk, and he still thinks there's money to be made. Now, if I show him the right approach, he'll be the easiest guy to sell.'"

"Dr. Smith?" says Chip picking up the phone to speak with a potential client. His voice has the all-American ring of someone brought up on the legend of George Washington and the cherry tree. He's also acquired a slight southern accent along the way. "You and I talked about six months ago about managed commodity accounts. You asked me to call you back in early '83."

Chip pauses while Dr. Smith tells him he can't recall the conversation. "Have a complete blank, huh?" says Chip still undaunted. "Are you trading commodities?" (Pause.) "Have you ever?" (Pause.) "No interest in them?" Dr. Smith makes vague mention of something once bought on paper. Chip slips through the opening and starts talking at the speed of light.

In offices throughout the newly renovated East Dallas mansion that serves as the company's headquarters, other young brokers are making similiar calls. At least they better be. "She started with her normal routine of making thirty to forty calls a day," said Chip of a woman who recently joined his company after leaving her job as a broker in a major commodity firm. "She would come in at nine and leave at 3:00 P.M. So I said, 'You're not leaving here until I see you dial the phone a hundred times.' I said, 'If you don't make fifty grand this year, we're going to fire you.'"

The former national sales manager for IBM is coming to work for Chip, and Chip's already worried that he'll be satisfied making "only" a hundred thousand dollars a year. "He's got a Rolls, he's got a balloon, he's got a nice house, he's got a gorgeous wife. Some people are satisfied at a certain level."

At what level would Chip be satisfied? "I want ten guys who are so sharp they will personally make a million dollars a year each, right here inside this 'little shack,'" Chip said. "If they're making a million, I'm making a million off of each of them, plus the value of the company, plus the trading of our own accounts. I might settle for that."

There probably weren't many other senior class presidents in high school in 1978 who were suspended by the school administration twice during their term of office. Chip was, and the reason had something to do with "contrary opinion," to use that commodities term again. Chip had a problem with authority.

The suspensions came within weeks of each other. The first one occurred in the high school cafeteria when Chip confronted a classmate who was dating his sister and had struck her. "I was very calm," Chip recalled. "I said, 'Don't hit my sister.' He said, 'I'll do whatever I damn well please.' And I went wham! He went out cold. So I got a week's vacation, which I needed."

Soon after returning to school Chip was called upon to perform the most important function of the senior class president: to organize the senior class party. Already an expert in two commodities—barley and hops—Chip realized the party would be dreary unless it had the secret ingredient of all successful high school bashes—beer. It goes without saying that there was a regulation against having liquor on school property. Chip would probably have obeyed the rule, except that someone bet him that he couldn't find some way to sneak beer into school.

"You know Pepsi Light? It's a blue can with a yellow stripe," Chip said. "Well, we decided to get about twenty cases of Pepsi Light and two hundred cases of beer and to take the beer to a body shop and paint them to look identical to the Pepsi Light. They came out perfect."

Chip and his partners in crime backed a van up to the one-acre, indoor student center, where all one thousand members of the senior class had assembled, and started passing out "Pepsi Light." Word spread fast. "About two hundred people came running up and mobbed the truck," Chip recalled with pride. "And the teachers who were there to monitor our activities started to wonder, 'Why is this crowd dashing for Pepsi Light?' We had been careful to hand the teachers real Pepsi Light. They got wind of the fact there was beer, and we were busted."

It seems only fair that Chip was suspended during his class presidency, since his original campaign for class president—SPEAK OUT WITH FICHTNER—was based on his defiant attitude toward authority. "My campaign speech was on the speak-out theory," Chip said. "'We're the democracy of this school just like the people of this country are a democracy.' I wrote it in the car on the way over." No doubt while driving.

Chip easily beat all the professional student government preppies who ran against him. Probably part of the reason he ran was to enjoy the looks on their faces after he vanquished them. Chip was a non-preppy. He hung out with the guys at the "industrial arts" end of the educational spectrum, guys who played with their cars instead of going to class. In his school uniform, a green gas-station attendant's jacket and grease-stained overalls, you'd never have guessed that both Chip's father and grandfather attended Harvard.

Whether you consider Chip a bully and a braggart or a ballsy idealist probably depends on whether or not you're standing in his way. To his friends, he can be enormously loyal, compassionate, and generous. "Chip was never a bully until someone crossed his ego," says Grant Curtis, a high school friend. "He had the sense that he was the big guy. He just didn't take any crap from anybody under any circumstances."

"I have a deep sense of fairness," Chip explained. "And if somebody's not being fair I'll step in. If somebody's trying to cheat somebody else, I'll step in, even if it's none of my business."

Chip keeps in touch with many of his old friends from high school. It's not hard for him to do, since most of them work for him. When he needed a construction foreman to supervise the renovation of several of his properties, he called Jim Wolffer, who had been in the trucking business, another high school venture, with Chip. Jim was at the University of North Carolina, only hours away from getting his diploma, and he offered to come to Dallas after he graduated in December. "I said, 'No, Jim, we need you now,'" recalled Chip who pulled strings to have Jim complete his schooling in Dallas. "Jim's trustworthy as hell," Chip added. "And he's a great get-it-done tiger."

At the end of the workday, Chip's army assembles in his office to drink Coors and listen to Chip hold court. Those who have known him since high school say the most obvious way he's changed is that he's developed a sense of style. On a recent morning, Chip purchased five custom-made suits and twenty Brooks Brothers shirts. Also, he no longer snubs the establishment on principle and enjoys dining at the finest restaurants with local politicians, press agents, and members of Dallas society.

Still, it's not as if Chip shuns his old friends. "It's a weakness of Chip's. He'll put everybody on the payroll," a friend says. Chip's paternalistic attitude extends even to his family. His father, a corporate retirement planner, worked in Washington five days a week for many years, while his mother and younger sister and brother continued to live in Connecticut. "He adores my mom and my grandmother," said Chip's sister Christie. "And he feels protective of both of them. Chip always felt my mom was alone a lot, which she was." Chip's parents have enough money to buy whatever they want, but recently Chip bought both of them cars.

His generosity towards women friends is legendary. It is not unusual for him to spend hundreds of dollars a month on a girlfriend. He bought a car for one woman he dated for several years, and when she tired of it, he bought her a more expensive car. He took her to Hawaii and gave her credit cards and clothes. For all his generosity, she dumped him on his birthday for a fraternity brother. Whether Chip felt the pain in his ego or his heart, he was devasted. A friend was traveling around the world at the time, and Chip reached him on a boat in the middle of the ocean. He just wanted a shoulder to cry on.

Such displays are rare for Chip. "He's very giving and caring to family members, but affection scares him," Christie said. "It's hard to go up and give him a hug. He's so stern. He feels he has to be strong and tough."

Christie said it was only recently that Chip revealed to his parents his resentment at having to carry a gray, utilitarian lunch box to school as a child, while all the other kids used colorful boxes with cartoon characters on them. "It was so typical of him that he never seemed to care," Christie said. "It was in him and he thought about it, but he never asked for anything."

Chip's ranch, with its motorcycles, hot tubs, cars, horses, half-a-dozen Labrador retrievers, and the TV tuned to cartoons every Saturday morning, seems nothing so much as a man-sized playground. His parents recently gave him a giant, stuffed Bugs Bunny for Christmas and a lunch box with cartoon characters.

"His family offers a lot of encouragement to be somebody, to be successful," a friend observed.

"We call them the three B's," said Chip's father referring to his children. "Chip is the brains; his sister Christie, an international fashion model, is the beauty; and his younger brother Dean, a high school swimming champion, is the brawn."

If Chip has role models, it's less his father than his grandfather, who supported his own mother when he was ten after his father died. Another role model is Chip's uncle Bob Walker. Chip jokingly refers to Bob as "my arch rival." According to Grant, Bob is one of the fifty richest men in Texas.

"I emulate him far more than I rival him," Chip said. "He's been extremely successful because he's worked his backside off."

"Chip tries to compete with Bob," a friend observed. "Right now they're not even on the same scale. But twenty years from now, Chip'll give Bob a run for his money. Chip's ultimate goal is to control more wealth and have more 'toys' than anybody else."

Toys are important to Chip. They are symbols of success to himself and to the outside world. "My problem is I can spend everything I make and more, a lot more," Chip said without sounding worried. "I'm addicted to toys. I have to keep my toy fleet up. The only thing my banker ever turned me down on a loan for was a caboose. It was cheap, only $5,000. But he said, 'No. You don't need a caboose. You've got enough toys.'

"I just want to be able to buy all the toys I want to buy," he added. "If I want to buy a new Lear Jet I want to be able to buy a new Lear Jet." Chip already has his eye out for a good used one, but once he gets it he'll probably be satisfied with it for just under ten minutes. He can already tell you what you can get a good used 727 for, and why a 747 isn't worth the hassle. "They take too much gas, and you can't land them where you want to land them," Chip said.

"Chip lives extended," explained a friend and business associate. "It's an incentive to keep going, to keep producing, keep expanding. If you're like Chip, you're never going to be late paying a bill. You're just going to figure out a way and work a little harder."

Kathy
Gallagher

Photo by Mark Hofmann

*E*nter *Kathy Gallagher's restaurant in Beverly Hills any* evening, and there's a good chance you'll see Johnny Carson, Warren Beatty, or a dozen other members of Hollywood royalty. But the focus of most of the attention, the reason people come to this restaurant instead of all the others that line the posh drives and canyons of Los Angeles, is the hostess herself.

In a town where restaurants use unlisted numbers to attract business, Kathy Gallagher's is a place that allows people to let down their facades. The reason is Kathy Gallagher.

"When it comes to interacting with people, Kathy has no peer," said Jim McMullen, Kathy's former fiancé and owner of a similarly fast-track restaurant in New York. "She's perfect for this business. She creates a certain excitement in a room that nobody else can duplicate."

"You've got to look at a restaurant as a place of entertainment," explained Patrick Terrail, Kathy's current beau, and proprietor of Ma Maison, one of Los Angeles's most elegant restaurants. "A person feels very comfortable in the tumult that takes place in Kathy's restaurant."

A young lawyer who eats there twice a week had no trouble describing what draws him to Kathy Gallagher's. "There are incredibly beautiful girls here, they're all her friends. The reason the place is so successful is because it has a party feeling instead of a bar feeling. If you've been there a few times she'll come up to you, and ask you how you've been. She's not pretentious. She doesn't make you feel as if you're not good enough to be there."

The core of Kathy's crowd consists of young people on their way up in Hollywood—junior studio executives, entertainment lawyers, semi-employed actors and actresses, and models, models, models. Drop by any night and you might also see Steve Martin stuffing his face at table #5 or Warren Beatty.

More than likely there's a bachelor party going on in the banquet room upstairs. It was there that Desi Arnaz, Jr., and Billy Hinsche hired a stripper and belly dancer to bid a not very tearful farewell to Dean Paul Martin before he skated off into the sunset with Olympian Dorothy Hamill. Kathy's is where Dino, Desi, and Billy held their weekly "boys' night out." Quite simply, it's the best saloon in Tinseltown.

Everyone advised Kathy not to open a restaurant in Los Angeles. She had moved there from New York only months before, after breaking up with Jim McMullen. And though McMullen's restaurant, which she helped him start, had proved her brilliant in the "front of the house"—restaurant lingo for greeting guests at the door and guiding them to a table—she was untested in the "back of the house"—managing the kitchen, hiring and firing employees, and balancing the books.

McMullen bought out her share of his restaurant. It was a

lot of money, especially for a young woman who came from an Irish Catholic working-class background in Maryland. To start a restaurant of her own, she'd have to spend every penny of her settlement and borrow an additional hundred thousand dollars from the bank. It was the kind of gamble that would have made a professional poker player sweat.

"The restaurant business is a very iffy thing," explained Robert Cohen, a restaurant lawyer who represented Kathy in her negotiations with McMullen. "It's a very expensive ordeal. More people go into bankruptcy than not. So as a professional I said, 'Kathy, you've worked so hard. You've got all this money. Why don't you think of clipping coupons for a while."

All the stories that were written about Jim and Kathy focused on the facts that Kathy was a model and Jim's fiancée; that they were building their very own love nest on Third Avenue in Manhattan, and that the nest just happened to seat several hundred people. Whenever the restaurant was written up it was Jim who was quoted.

"It was important to me that people knew I was strong and that I didn't need Jim to do it," said Kathy, explaining why she ignored all the negative advice and went ahead with her restaurant. She still wears the large engagement diamond Jim gave her, but she's had it reset in a man's gold pinky ring. "I could have done anything I wanted. I could have gone to Europe and lived for a year. I could have gone back to school. But it was like, 'I'm going to do this and it's going to be great.'"

Though Kathy severed her emotional bonds to Jim, she stuck closely to the formula that had made McMullen's one of the most successful restaurants in Manhattan. Like McMullen's, her restaurant would be named after the owner who would be there to greet her guests. The decor would be simple and natural, and there would be flowers everywhere, first-class food, and lots of beautiful people.

She recruited her twenty-five-year-old brother from Maryland to run the "back of the house" while she composed the dining space as if it were a painting—everything from tables to lighting to toothpicks. "She was trying to carbon-copy McMullen's because she had a fear of varying that success," said Patrick Terrail. "I've had an ongoing, amusing argument with her about putting a blender in the bar. She refuses to do it because she says every drink they had at McMullen's was shaken. In California, we have mixed drinks, like strawberry and banana daiquiris, which are big money-makers. But she refuses to use a blender. Her nemesis is Jim McMullen's but her asset at the same time is Jim McMullen's."

Kathy has a few assets all her own. She has a heightened sense of aesthetics that is evident in everything from the way she dresses to the way she artfully arranges the flowers she picks out herself at the flower market to the way the food is arranged on the plate.

"She has her personal touch on every dish that goes out," observed Jody Briskin, the restaurant's manager. "And when she's doing a Sunday brunch, she doesn't just leave it to the chef. She has a very definite eye on how she wants the food to look.

"I've seen her take someone who's been there a long, long time, someone she is very fond of, and say, 'You knew I wouldn't like this vegetable. Why did you make it?'"

Another one of her assets is dedication. Though she lives in a two-bedroom house with a swimming pool in the heart of Beverly Hills and has a newly purchased Mercedes, Kathy rarely gets to enjoy her possessions. "She works all the time," said Kathy's best friend, Linda Lloyd. "If she's out of the restaurant one whole night and one half night a week, that's a lot." Restaurant regulars are only half joking when they ask Kathy if she lives above the restaurant.

Kathy's greatest asset may be her ability to market herself. "I was getting written up before I even opened. In this town, though, there's a lot to write about celebrities, after a while they need something else to write about," said Kathy sitting at "her table," the one to which she invites her personal guests. "This was definitely something new in the area—a twenty-seven-year-old woman opening her own restaurant with no partners. Every restaurant here has tons of partners."

At the same time Kathy was dating Donald Pliner, the owner of a chic clothing store on Rodeo Drive—Beverly Hills's most fashionable strip of commercial real estate— and one of the city's most eligible and visible bachelors.

Whenever there was a charity benefit or a movie premiere, there would almost certainly be a picture in the paper the next day of Kathy, blond and impeccable, on Pliner's arm. In response to a local paper's inquiring photographer's question, "What is one thing you do extremely well?" Pliner answered, "Falling in love with Kathy Gallagher."

"She's great at her own PR," observed Jody Briskin. "She's always at the right places. She always gets people into the restaurant. A lot of times there will be a big charity function and a lot of our customers will be there. They like to see Kathy outside the restaurant so they can chat with her."

In Hollywood, the cognoscenti say they're on their way to "Kathy's" as if they were just dropping by somebody's home. Inevitably, the first question out of their mouths after they walk through the door is, "Where's Kathy?"

She caters to celebrities just like every other "hot" restaurant in Los Angeles, but she does so more casually than places which have an unlisted telephone number and treat people who haven't been nominated for an Oscar lately like delivery boys.

Still, Kathy's been in the restaurant business long enough to know that if it's reported that Johnny Carson had dinner there the night before, business will pick up at lunch. When Steve Martin appears, he's escorted straight to table #5. "He's a very easygoing guy but that's where we'd put someone"—Kathy is too discreet to use the word "famous"—"because it's one of the better tables and people are seen there. Regular customers know there's usually someone interesting at that table."

Warren Beatty always calls in advance to have a table reserved for him. It's in the rear of the restaurant by a door. "If he's with a date, they'll usually go out the back way. If he's with the guys he'll go out the front door."

What's remarkable about the restaurant is that it manages to stroke celebrities' egos without forsaking the ambience that makes a young lawyer or architect feel completely comfortable. It's only on second glance that you realize that the man brooding over a menu at a table in the bar area is actually a piece of sculpture. Apart from its impact as a conversation piece, the sculpture transmits a message:

Kathy Gallagher isn't so greedy that she has to squeeze a buck out of every available inch of floor space.

"In this town you realize people can be fascinated with you today and you can be gone tomorrow," Linda Lloyd said. "In terms of the social climbing that goes on here, there are the *A, B,* and *C* groups. There really are lists that have these people's names on it. But Kathy's not really interested in any of that. They accept her. If they want to invite her to their parties then she's happy to go. If not, she doesn't spend a lot of time worrying about it."

Kathy was crowned Miss Gateway, 1969. Gateway was the name of the local club patronized by the well-to-do families in the Washington, D.C., suburb where she lived. Kathy wasn't one of them but, "I wasn't looking to hang out in my neighborhood, obviously," she recalled.

Her parents divorced when she was only six, and Kathy and her younger brother and sister were raised by their mother. The idea that a woman works to support herself comes naturally to Kathy. She worked as an in-house model at a local department store throughout high school and started entering beauty pageants when she was sixteen. "I guess being in beauty pageants was a way of getting out of the mold I was in of going to the Catholic girl's school and dating the boy from the Catholic boy's school," she said.

Though she was pretty and could have played the field, Kathy was never boy-crazy, according to her mother. She was always serious, committed. She dated the same boy from the time she was thirteen until she graduated from high school. His name was Bill McCullough, not to be confused with Jim McMullen, but he fit the same general description. "He had a beautiful family," Kathy recalled. "He was the most popular kid in his grade, blond and cute."

A photographer who met Kathy at a beauty pageant needed a model to pose for his portfolio and asked Kathy to do it. When he went to New York and tried to peddle his work, the modeling agencies weren't interested. But his model caught their eye. "They called me on the spot," remembered Kathy, who was about to start her freshman year at Prince George's Community College in Maryland. "They said, 'Would you come up for an interview?' It was in the afternoon. I can't remember what I was doing. I can just remember my hair flying up from jumping."

The agency, Stewart Models, accepted her on the spot. Kathy called her mother and told her to get back her college registration fee. She earned a living as a model and quickly got into TV commercials. Shampoo and toothpaste ads were her specialty. "'Gee, your hair smells terrific,' it might have been Jergens," said Kathy trying to remember an early ad as if she were trying to recall a previous life. "I did Super-Max hair dryer, Delco batteries, and two Close-Up toothpaste ads." Kathy's teeth are flawless; she never wore braces.

"I was just determined to be a success," she said. "I had an image of myself that way. There are ways it could have been easier for me by marrying someone rich or famous. But I'm not interested. It's probably the values I got while growing up. How could I be trustworthy if I was cheap enough to give myself away to get something for it?

"I could have found someone to give me the money to do all this," she added, referring to the restaurant, "but it would have made me not want to do it as much."

Kathy met Jim McMullen when they were cast as boyfriend and girlfriend in an ad. "Jim and I were both the All-American types. We were considered a junior market. As opposed to a *Vogue* model, which is a kind of high-fashion, sophisticated look, we were 'cutesy.'"

The next time Kathy saw Jim was in Bloomingdale's a couple of months later. He didn't recognize her. "I recognized him," Kathy recalled. "I said, 'Hi, how are you?' But as I'm into the second or third sentence, I realize this guy doesn't know who I am. Women were on his fingertips all the time."

They ended up having dinner that night and for many nights to follow. He made me laugh and we had a good time," she said. They modeled by day, often as boyfriend and girlfriend in the ads as well as in real life, and did the East Side bar scene by night.

Kathy and Jim became convinced they could open a successful restaurant themselves. Jim was already in his late twenties, and even though he was making a lot of money modeling, he was eager to start a business that would support him after his boyish features had faded. "We knew enough people in the business and, being models, we certainly had the means to get a lot of people in quickly. It's the only basis on which we went into the restaurant," Kathy recalled.

The restaurant was called Harper's. "We were busy right off the bat," Kathy said. "As soon as you'd start reading such and such model was seen eating at Harper's, you'd fill the bar immediately."

Harper's was so instantly successful that Jim sold his share and moved to larger quarters up the street. Kathy had a minority share in the new restaurant, but it was still Jim's name that went on the awning, and it was Jim who gave the interviews to reporters and restaurant critics. Jim transformed Kathy and himself from carefree models into the swingingest Mom and Pop in town. "It's a simple, family-oriented restaurant," Jim told one interviewer. "We figured there weren't too many of them in this city." A *Daily News* caption under a picture of them hugging for the cameras read, "Kathy Gallagher and Jim McMullen find the happiness they always dreamed of in front of their new restaurant."

"We were engaged," Jim explained. "We discussed all of the decisions. We worked in the restaurant. I owned more stock than she did, but we were about to get married."

Despite the "Mom and Pop" hype, McMullen's attracted some of the most unattached characters in town. The regulars included Reggie Jackson, Jimmy Connors, Vitas Gerulaitis (who routinely parked his Rolls-Royce in front of a fire hydrant across the street), and bushels of the most beautiful models in town. From the start, the restaurant was a smash. They even sold out for lunch.

Unfortunately Jim and Kathy's relationship didn't fare as well as the restaurant. "It's a demanding business and it takes its toll on personal relationships," Jim said. "You always have to be nice to everybody you're with. Sometimes the person you care about the most is the person who gets abused the most."

It was Kathy who moved out, but Jim didn't try to stop her. "To this day we have a hard time talking to each other," Kathy said.

"I felt like I was fighting for the first two years," she said. "I had to go through a lot of learning and it was hard for me to break through some old thoughts I had."

Sometimes she's even able to relax. This summer she's planning to take a month off and rent a beach house in East Hampton, Long Island, with Cynthia Sikes, star of the TV show "St. Elsewhere."

Kathy described the qualities she admired in Cynthia; she might as well have been describing herself. "She has star quality," Kathy said. "She's very together, very into her career. She's not messing around, not doing it for ego. She's doing it for business. It's very important for her to make that kind of money."

Kathy said the difference between Cynthia and her is that Kathy is still at the point where her restaurant is, "half ego, half business. By next year it's going to be more money for me. It gets to the point where you satisfy your ego. If you're going to stay with it, because it is very hard, it's really got to be taking you somewhere."

"I'm at a point where I know I'm successful at what I'm doing, and I'm anxious to do more," she said. "And once I feel good about that, I'll probably be ready to settle down. It's like, I've got to take care of this first."

"There are people who are successful because they walk on the right side of the road," said Kathy's lawyer Robert Cohen. "That's not my sense of why Kathy has the success she has. I think there's something inside her that really motivates her. That woman's not going to have one restaurant. She's going to have dozens of restaurants. She's going to have her name in a lot of cities."

"I think this is just the beginning of what she's going to do," Jim McMullen said. "I wouldn't be surprised if she ends up in politics."

Kathy is currently writing a recipe/menu cookbook for Macmillan Publishers. She would also like to open a couple of other restaurants and make a lot more money. She says she's not interested in starting a chain of restaurants. It goes against her sense of aesthetics. "Everything becomes so patterned and pre-fab looking," she said.

But she realizes the Hollywood community holds her to the same bone-crunching standards of success by which they judge each other. "It's good for your customers to know you're successful," Kathy observed. "They want to be where it's real successful. I'm not dealing with a movable clientele.

It's not like there are tourists coming here. My presence wouldn't be important to them."

"Women like to be around her because she's a good sign of the females of our time," Jody Briskin explained. "It's like, 'Look, we can be successful. We can be on our own and yet be very feminine,' and I think that's why we get such a large ladies' crowd. It's a good sign for femininity."

There's another reason they get such a large ladies' crowd, at least on Tuesday night. Tuesday night is "Ladies' Night." "Women who come in with their girlfriends get all the free champagne they can drink," Briskin explained. "The only requirement is that they don't bring any guys."

Joe Kennedy II

*T*he Nigerians demanded a $750,000 performance bond before they'd sign a multimillion dollar oil contract with Citizens Energy Corporation, Joe Kennedy II's Boston-based, non-profit oil company. It was already 2:00 P.M. on a Friday, and getting a check for three-quarters of a million dollars in Nigeria before the banks closed at 5:00 P.M. was about as easy as walking on water.

"Joe said he'd go out and scout up the money at the local Chase bank," recalled Wilber James, the vice-president of Citizens Energy. "He got in a cab and came back two hours later with a check for $750,000. The Nigerians were absolutely incredulous. They kept looking at the check, turning it over to see what kind of counterfeit he'd brought back.

We've become very close to Nigeria since then. They refer to Joe as Muhammad. The mountain came to Muhammad."

The analogy may not be that far off. Joe Kennedy II, the eldest son of Ethel and the late Senator Robert F. Kennedy, is a David competing against Goliaths, a man who at the age of twenty-seven rallied his vast resources—charm, chutzpah, family connections, arrogance, and hundred-horsepower ambition—to establish an oil company to supply low-cost heating fuel to poor people in Massachusetts. He is also arranging financial backing for landlords who insulate their run-down buildings, tax breaks for consumers who donate leftover heating oil to the poor, and funding for experimental energy projects in third world countries.

It would probably have been impossible for anyone other than a Kennedy to get such a pie-in-the-sky project off the ground, but that shouldn't lessen Joe's achievement. Probably no other Kennedy of his generation could have made Citizens Energy succeed. Forget about the family for a second and look at the man. At the age of thirty, barrel-chested and an occasional bully, yet acutely sensitive to people's suffering, Joe Kennedy is larger than life. If any actor were to portray him in a movie, it would have to be a young Marlon Brando.

"He's unusual, never mind his age," said Parkman Clancy, a consultant to Citizens Energy and a former executive at Gulf Oil. "He's willing to joust with damn near anything that comes his way."

The offices of Citizens Energy are on the third floor of a building that faces the Massachusetts State House. They were first rented by John F. Kennedy in 1946 and have been used by one Kennedy or another ever since. A watercolor of the late president sailing a small boat hangs over the couch in the makeshift reception area. A sense of purpose is almost tangible here as young people in jackets and ties move in and out of offices, as teletypes and typewriters clatter away. Joe frequently sticks his head out of his office, intercepts an assistant, and demands information or answers. "He's got to be on the phone or he's got to be doing something," said one of Joe's business associates. "That's part of the energy, calling people up and saying, 'What's happening? Why isn't something happening?'"

Joe's office is furnished with third- and fourth-hand furniture but it still has the feel of an executive suite. Business is conducted standing up or sitting on the couch. A desk in the corner that looks like it came from a kindergarten is filled with framed photographs of Joe's three-year-old twin boys. It's obvious that Kennedy is no good at sitting at desks. While being interviewed, he continuously shifts his weight back and forth and kicks the coffee table whenever the questions touch on his personal life.

"I was over at my friend Dick Goodwin's house with my wife, Sheila, a few years ago," said Joe tracing the origins of Citizens Energy. Richard Goodwin was an adviser to Joe's father. "The television was on and they were showing the billions of dollars the oil companies were making. At the same time it was the middle of winter and people were suffering. It was actually Dick who said, 'What would happen if you started an organization that took those billions of dollars and turned it back to the people?' I think that's how he put it."

Joe had worked on fund raising for the Kennedy Library and had run his uncle Teddy's 1976 Senate campaign, but he'd never initiated a venture. Unprecedented as the idea may have seemed it was tailor-made for Kennedy. It smacked of the impossible dream, demanded extraordinary energy and devotion, and was a chance to go one-on-one with the powers that be.

Joe and Steve Rothstein, a twenty-four-year-old Williams graduate whom Joe met on his uncle's Senate campaign, set up shop in the basement of Joe's home in the Brighton section of Boston. They spent six months boning up on the oil industry, rented a post office box to give the enterprise an official-looking address, and persuaded a friend to let them forward calls to her office where she picked up the phone and made believe she was their secretary.

"Basically, Steve and I got the names and addresses of about fifteen countries," Joe said. They wrote to nations such as Venezuela, Nigeria, and Ecuador, explaining that poor Americans froze during the winter and needed their oil. They slanted their appeals as much to the public relations instincts of those countries, as to any altruistic impulses. Joe reiterated what these countries already knew:

that every time OPEC raised its prices, American oil companies would tack an additional 15 percent onto the price at the pump and blame the increase on OPEC. Later, Joe also offered to reinvest 25 percent of the profits from Citizens Energy in the form of alternate energy projects in the supplier country or in a mutually agreed upon developing nation. "I wrote them that we could send a message to people and bring about greater understanding between the producing countries and the consuming countries."

A few countries replied—hesitantly. "They'd write back a letter and it would have fifteen conditions attached to it," Joe recalled. If Kennedy could get refineries to process the oil, tankers to ship it, ports to store it, and banks to cover the deal with letters of credit, nations such as Venezuela would sell him the oil. There were a lot of ifs.

Here's where the Kennedy connections came in handy. "If Joe Blow calls somebody up and says, 'I want to talk to the chairman of this or the vice-president of that because I've got an idea,' they're going to have a pretty rough time," explained a business associate who helped Joe get Citizens Energy off the ground. "They're generally put down at the bottom of the list and they have to work their way up. And the farther out the idea, the harder it is to work your way up the chain of command. So it's opening doors and entree. It's a chance to explain what you're up to. The name Kennedy doesn't hurt.

"But the whole operation doesn't depend on that on a continuing basis," the man added. "It depends on some real hard facts of life in the oil business. Nobody is going around and saying, 'Let's be awfully nice to this guy.' The oil business doesn't work that way."

The chairman of the board of Boston's Northeast Petroleum Oil Company, a college classmate of Joe's uncle Teddy, invited Joe to a meeting. "After the meeting, my chief executive said, 'What do you think you can do to help him?'" recalled John Buckley, the vice-president of Northeast Petroleum, who also attended the lunch. "Joe asked us who he should contact in this area; so we gave him a list of all the people, and he went out and saw them all himself."

Kennedy did the same thing throughout the world, visiting chief executives of shipping companies and refineries, and even a few heads of state. He spent thousands of hours and dollars crisscrossing the globe trying to put the deal together.

"So I had all these ducks lined up," Kennedy said. "I'd go get all fifteen conditions filled so that finally the last thing I had to get was Venezuela's agreement to sell us the crude."

The long awaited call from Venezuela came late one Friday afternoon in 1979. Joe was in Caracas Monday morning. "They had a very simpatico feeling for the Kennedy name, because his uncle Jack started the Alliance for Progress," said John Buckley. "Still, it took a good deal of skill to bring a contract to fruition. And Joe had that skill. He handles negotiations well. He handles people well. If he runs into an obstacle he facets on it and finds a way to get around it."

The deal Kennedy signed called for Venezuela to sell Citizens Energy 10,000 barrels of oil a day. It was worth over $100 million. "We have lifted every single barrel of crude oil we have ever contracted for," Joe stated proudly. "It's all done on time, paid for on time; so the business piece of it is very, very much in place."

The way the business works is that Joe buys the crude oil at full price from nations like Venezuela and ships it to refineries. Citizens Energy then sells the refined products, such as gasoline, diesel oil, and jet fuel, to the refinery and uses the profits to reduce the cost of the heating oil shipped to Massachusetts by as much as 40 percent below market rates. Wilbur James estimates Citizens has saved the citizens of the Bay State between $6 and $8 million over the four years the company has been in existence.

Still, Joe is scrambling these days. He's as adversely affected by the oil glut as Exxon or Shell. "I'd love to be able to expand Citizens Energy into other areas," said Joe. "It's easy to talk about when you make five dollars a barrel on imported crude oil. On the other hand, when there's a two to three dollar loss on every barrel it's hard to think in an expanding mode."

Hard but not impossible, and Citizens Energy continues to branch out faster than ivy on a Beacon Hill townhouse. The reinvestment program has already built the largest solar energy system in the Caribbean: in Jamaica, where it's providing hot water to a hospital that couldn't afford it before. CEC has also brought electricity to a remote region of Costa Rica by refining "biomass," a futuristic term for cow manure, and using the energy-rich methane gas which comes from it.

"HOT," Home Oil Transfer, offers tax deductions to people who donate leftover oil to the Robert F. Kennedy Memorial after they've converted from oil to some other energy source. Joe got the idea from a man who wrote asking why he imported thousands of barrels of oil from foreign countries when the man has a hundred gallons sitting in his basement.

The program has spread to nine utility areas in four states—New York, Massachusetts, New Jersey, and Pennsylvania—and it's on its way to Canada.

In 1981, Citizens Energy started the Citizens Conservation Corporation which is designed to conserve energy in apartment buildings occupied by low-income and elderly families. Landlords pay CCC what they used to pay in fuel bills. In exchange, Kennedy's people perform an extensive energy audit, weatherize the building, conduct tenant education seminars, and pay the fuel bill. The average heat loss in Massachusetts old housing is 35 percent. "If you save 35 percent of the energy, that's a lot of money to cover expenses," explained Steve Rothstein, Kennedy's soft-spoken aide-de-camp.

Joe met Wilber James, the nuts-and-bolts brains behind Citizens Energy, when Joe visited Kenya in 1970 to film an *American Sportsman* episode. Wilber was working as a Peace Corps volunteer teaching agricultural techniques to the Watharaka, a primitive tribe that hunted with poison-tipped arrows. Wilber lived on beans, corn, canned goods, and water kept cold by a kerosene refrigerator in his tent. Elephants, lions, and twenty-five-foot pythons hunted within sight of the tribe. Hyenas ate Wilber's soap. The only other white man in the area was a missionary who lived fifteen miles away.

"The American ambassador knew of me," said Wilber. "I had a unique living environment with this tribe. So he introduced me to Joe, and Joe asked to come out, and he lived there for several months.

"I don't know how many days we spent in the same tent,"

added Wilber, twisting his handlebar moustache, "but it was a long time. Maybe it was a week, but it was not an easy week. Joe can be very abrasive. He was disruptive because he's got a lot of energy to burn and he asked a lot of questions. So eventually he got his own tent." For four months Joe worked beside the tribesmen installing machinery and removing rocks from the fields.

Joe was useful to Wilber not only as a source of manpower, but also because he attracted high-level attention to the plight of the tribe. "Several times we met some very famous Kenyans," Wilber recalled. "They were attracted to Joe Kennedy—people like the president and vice-president of the country." But socializing was not the rule, and when *Life* magazine wanted to do a story on the Watharaka, Wilber and Joe turned them down. "They said they wanted to do a story on me and the tribe," Wilber said, "but it was obvious they wanted to do a story on Joe Kennedy with the tribe and this Peace Corps volunteer."

Joe returned home a few months later. "I assumed I'd see him again," Wilber said, "but it wasn't a given. I didn't know if I'd live in Africa for the rest of my life."

But after several bouts with malaria, Wilber was forced to return to the States. He became a VISTA worker and later a successful real estate entrepreneur in Seattle. When Joe started Citizens Energy, consultants told him he wasn't going to be able to run the company on charm and connections. He needed someone to run the day-to-day organization while he globe-trotted. Joe called Wilber, his jack-of-all-trades. "I came back and looked at the thing for a week and told him what needed to be done," Wilber recalled. "If Joe decides that this person is right for the job, he's pretty convinced that's the person for the job and nobody else. He kept bugging me. I said I'd come back for a couple of months to help out, and I've been here four years."

"What motivates people to join Joe's bandwagon?" asked a Kennedy associate rhetorically. "I think it's a combination of things. Joe's not an easy guy to work for. On the other hand he's very, very charming when he wants to be. There's also got to be the question of idealism that attracts people to this sort of caper."

Kennedy talks about the state of the world the way other

people talk about the siding on their homes. Maybe it's just
that carrying the weight of the world around on one's shoulders is the family business but you don't have to listen to
Joe long before you start to ask yourself, "What have I done
for the planet today?"

Since Wilber began to work for Joe, their friendship has
deepened, and Wilber's respect for Joe has grown. "What
made Citizens Energy work was Joe Kennedy," stated Wilber. "First of all he's smart. People don't believe he's smart
because he doesn't have a Master's or a PhD. But he's got
incredible street sense. He's very intuitive regarding people.
He knows whether somebody is telling him the truth or not.
He can cut through the bullshit very quickly, probably better than anybody I've ever met. He doesn't like to take no for
an answer, and he's not intimidated by anyone."

An incident in Algeria shows just how principled Joe can
be. He flew in to sign an oil deal with the Algerians, but
when he arrived they informed him that the prices had gone
up. "We had a meeting over there and I thought we were
going to start throwing chairs," recalled one of the partici-
pants. "Joe was not only disappointed in their behavior,
which was patently bad, but he also resented that they were
at the same time putting on this face of being sympathetic
to his program. It was a session marked by a great deal of
explicit views on who was doing what to whom. And these
Algerian oil tycoons had taken over the role of playing god
for a while. They had not run across this before—somebody
told them what they thought of them fairly upfront." The
deal was never made.

People seem to think Joe gets his gladiatorial instincts
from his father. "It's obvious that somebody taught him
early on to get up front and hang tough," one associate said.

There's a photograph on Joe's desk of his father walking
on ahead while Joe, who couldn't have been more than ten
when the picture was taken, follows at a respectful distance, beaming. "I think he has very, very high regard for
his father," John Buckley said. "Obviously his father had a
very positive influence on him. I'm just saying that because
I see a lot of good in the guy, and it had to come from somewhere. And because he refers to his Dad with a very positive
kind of feeling. He's very proud of him."

If, as Wilber James said, some people don't believe Joe is smart, it's not for the lack of a PhD, but because of the reputation Joe developed when he was younger. He didn't excel academically at Milton Academy, and instead of going on to Harvard, which grabs Kennedys with the same gusto that some Southern colleges recruit high school football stars, Joe attended the University of Massachusetts.

"He only managed to hang in there because he was a Kennedy," commented a Milton classmate. "But he was the kind of character, well-bred, big, bubbly, who could have pulled his act together and done well in the real world."

Joe was also involved in two car accidents. In the first one, on the West Coast, only he was injured. But in the second in Nantucket in 1973, one of the passengers in his jeep, Pamela Kelly, was paralyzed for life when the vehicle overturned.

"People have written their own judgments about troubles I've faced going through high school," said Joe reflecting on his past. "I don't know if they're a lot different from the ones 95 percent of all the kids in this country grow up facing."

In 1979 Joe married Sheila Rauch, a housing specialist for the City of Boston. "Sheila's her own woman," said Joe proudly. "She's terrific, she's independent, and she takes care of our children. She's just great."

In 1980, Sheila gave birth to twin boys. One is named Joe and the other Matthew. Joe bought a farmhouse for his family on the south shore of Massachusetts, and he commutes to work by boat eight months of the year. "The most important thing in my life is really my family," he said. "My wife and my children. I'd like to hope that no matter what happens in terms of fame and fortune, those are the people that are important."

Joe doesn't see the success of Citizens Energy as proof that he's changed since high school. Just the opposite. It's his way of continuing to question authority. "As to whether the success of Citizens Energy has changed some of my basic attitudes," said Joe, his shoe starting to scrape self-consciously against the coffee table, "I hope it allows me to question authority and question a lot of other people's basic judgments about what's right for me, or what's right for people I know and love, or this state, or the country I live in.

I mean, screw them. That's still a part of me, and I think I'm realistic enough to recognize it."

Minutes after Teddy Kennedy announced he would not run for President in 1984, the telephones at Citizens Energy started to light up. The media was trying to take the political torch and pass it on to the next generation. Joe didn't take a single call. For now, he seems completely committed to Citizens Energy.

Still, politics is the air Joe breathes. His vision is so sweeping and his business so affected by international politics that he can't help but be politically astute. It may actually have been oil's hidden political allure that attracted him to it in the first place.

Politics sneaks up on Joe in other ways as well. Though he has met with Saudi Arabia's oil minister, Sheik Amad Zaki Yamani, Joe has had much difficulty doing business in the Middle East. "I suppose it has a lot to do with my Uncle's stand and support of the State of Israel," Joe said. "That's really what it comes down to."

When I asked Joe point-blank about his own political ambition, he seemed suddenly exasperated. "I hope this isn't another thing where Citizens Energy is a political launching pad," he said. "It's not a very good analogy."

But he certainly appreciates the platform the media offers him. At the dedication of the Kennedy Library on 20 October 1979, the *New York Times* reported, "The sharpest political language came not from the two probable rivals (Kennedy and Carter) but from Joseph P. Kennedy II, son of the late Robert F. Kennedy. His passionately delivered remarks contained more than a hint of an attack on the Carter Administration's policies."

"You had a heck of a collection of powerful people there that day," Joe recalled. "It seemed like maybe they ought to be reminded. Maybe we ought to remember that a lot of the contributions that made that library possible came not just from the individuals there that day, but also from the sweat and hard work of what is the backbone of this country, which is the working people."

Joe can exhibit all the grace of a front-runner himself. "We were checking out of a hotel in Houston and some guy came up to him and said, 'Hey, you look like a Kennedy. Are you?' And Joe said yes, and he sat there and talked to this guy," said a business associate who accompanied Joe on a business trip. "The guy just wandered by and it went way beyond what you would normally expect of somebody saying hello. Now maybe that's political ego. He's got that aspect of great personal charm, and I think it's sincere."

I asked Joe what he thought of the mythology the media manufactures around the Kennedy clan and asked him specifically for his reaction to a story which quoted a Kennedy campaign worker as stating, ". . . If Joe decides to run he'll be tough. When he's in a crowd, you can see the same looks on people's faces that you saw for his uncles and his father."

"There's nothing you can do except try to steel yourself against it," Joe said. "What the media makes they can break. As I said before, I don't like being in someone else's hands. I just don't like it at all. I can't stop them from saying it but I'm just not going to deal with it, acknowledge it, or be a part of it."

Joe also sees something positive in the public's obsession with the Kennedy family. "It shows the desire of the people to have somebody they can put their faith in," he said, "someone who will lead this country and take on the challenges that it faces, rather than just bowing to interest groups."

Other nations certainly perceive Joe as a political figure. In Algeria, "We got off the rear of the plane and were walking down the pavement into the terminal and nobody was there," Wilber recalled. "Pretty soon this whole delegation of people came running around. They were the heads of the government and some other political figures. That pretty much sums up a lot of our experiences."

"I think the average black African looks at the United States and sees a country where it really happened," said Joe, "where the people brought a true democracy to their country for the first time in history. It's such an inspiration. They believe so much in our system. On the other hand, they see these companies come in and just bilk them of everything they've got. So they just see a hell of a dilemma."

Joe wants American oil companies to develop the third world's natural resources, "but write laws that say that twenty years from now there's going to be an Angola national oil company that's going to own those wells. You're going to teach the people how to work those wells, and you're going to send them to our schools, because we have the best engineers in the world. So what you really do is go in and develop the greatest assets the country has on both sides."

I asked Joe if he's been brought up with this sense of global responsibility. "I'm not any great philosopher," he said, his body tensing beneath his blue blazer, buttondown shirt and blue knit tie, as yet another reporter tries to place him in a historical setting. It's hard not to. He looks like a hybrid of Bobby and Teddy. "I don't have any great philosophy about life. I just try and take it one day at a time. And I certainly don't believe that just because of who I am I have some special responsibility, but rather that every human being has a responsibility to be true to themselves.

"I just try to deal with today," he added, his glance wandering as if to let his listener know that if he had no further questions about Citizens Energy it was time for Joseph P. Kennedy II to get back to work. "The difficulties and the games and the phone calls and the relationships in the oil business are enough that I don't need the additional sort of philosophical time to develop those thoughts. I don't have that piece of me and no amount of questions is going to bring it out. It probably isn't there."

Kennedy says he only thinks hard about the future when he considers the possibility of Citizens Energy failing. "I suppose the basic fact is that when you're doing a quarter of a billion dollars a year worth of business and your basic assets are a telephone and a typewriter you're always going to be dancing through the raindrops, every single day and every single hour of the day.

"We try to provide concrete benefits to poor people and to elderly people, and as long as we can do that, fine. The day that stops we'll close the door, and if nobody ever hears of Joe Kennedy again, that'll be all right. I hope I'll be able to handle it."

Debbie Fields

*R*andy Fields, a financial consultant to Fortune 500 companies, has met some of the most competitive men in America. But he believes his wife, Debbie, founder of Mrs. Fields Cookies, Inc., one of the fastest growing store chains in the country, is more competitive than any of them. She's the most competitive person Randy has ever met.

"If I can't buy the couch I want because I don't have the money for it, I won't buy any couch," said Debbie, translating her titanic drive into an analogy any housewife can relate to. She insists she is first and foremost a homemaker and that her cookie stores take a back seat to Randy and her two daughters: Jessica, who is almost four, and Jenessa, who is eighteen months. She is also pregnant again. "I will have nothing in the house until I have the couch that I want. And I will get that couch."

With a hundred stores and dozens more in the works, Debbie can afford any couch she wants. "Her competition is not other directed, it's inner directed," Randy explains. "She has in her mind, in an almost Platonic sense, what the standard of excellence is, and she always keeps in mind what she is doing in relation to that standard."

What Debbie has done is little short of extraordinary. In 1976, at the age of nineteen and recently married to Randy, Debbie decided she wanted to share with the world the cookies she baked for herself and her friends. She asked Randy, who was ten years older and already a successful economist, to lend her $50,000 to open a store. "I had the vision to say that although she was crazy, it would be a great experience for her in terms of learning business," Randy said.

He invited his own financial advisor, a vice-president at the Bank of America, over for lunch, and asked for his assessment of the economic potential of Debbie's cookies. "She brought the cookies out for dessert and then returned to the kitchen," Randy recalls. "I said, 'What do you think?'"

At this point it ought to be mentioned that Debbie is physically stunning, and it wouldn't have taken much effort for a male banker of perhaps parochial attitudes to dismiss her as nothing more than a Barbie doll. "He said, 'Randy, it's obvious it's not going to be a great business, but the worst that's going to happen is you're going to lose $50,000 and, after all, it's a tax shelter.'"

Debbie used the same recipe in the store she'd used at home—"real butter, real chocolate, real vanilla." Nobody bought them. "People came by, they looked at the cookies, and they didn't buy them," Debbie remembers. "And I knew they were great.

"I decided the only way I can convince these people it's a good cookie is for them to eat the cookie. If the customers aren't going to come to me, I'm going to go to them. And I piled the cookies on my cookie sheet and I walked up and down the streets of downtown Palo Alto finding people and saying, 'Please would you just try these cookies?' And they tried them and loved them and followed me back to the store."

Debbie rarely has time to parade in front of the store any more, but hundreds of employees do from Honolulu to Manhattan. Randy, who presides over the financial end of the operation, projects that Debbie will have 100 more stores a year later.

"After ten stores, she needed me like a hole in the head," said Randy, responding to rumors that he's the brains behind the beauty. "When the banks ask, 'What happens if something happens to you?' I tell them, 'Just get a good financial officer and everything will be fine.' I said the part that can't be replaced is Debbie. She's the heart and soul of the business. I'm the calculator and the systems person. You can hire me. You can't hire a Debbie."

The Fieldses refuse to disclose profits but acknowledge that they donate approximately one quarter of their earnings to charity. This year that figure will well exceed $1 million.

Debbie says she makes her cookies for love, not money. "Most people would say, 'Debbie Fields is so successful because she's making lots of money,'" Debbie said. "That's not success in my mind. I'll tell you what true success is in terms of what my goal is. My goal is to build a company of people who really want to be there, who when they wake up in the morning say to themselves, 'We're going to go out and sell some cookies and make some customers happy, and we're going to do some really nice things for the world.' My goal is to create a company that is really excited about being there, about being a participant in life."

Debbie seems almost too good to be true. "Everybody thinks that when they first meet her," Randy said.

Debbie is the youngest of five highly competitive sisters. "She came from a family where it was difficult to please, so my guess is that her whole orientation is toward pleasing people," Randy said. They were not well-off financially. Debbie's father was a welder.

"My father really wanted to have a son, so I tried to be one," said Debbie, sitting in the living room of her comfortable California home. The Fields' primary residence is in Park City, Utah, where the company headquarters are located. They also have a house in Hawaii where the company test-kitchens are located; they spend three months a year there. "I wanted my father to feel like he could go out and play basketball with me," she added. "I was trying to give him at least a little bit of happiness."

At thirteen, Debbie was hired as the foul line ballcatcher for the Oakland Athletics baseball team. She was already a knockout. Debbie didn't catch many foul balls, but she tried awfully hard and made a lot of friends.

During high school she worked in public relations for a local department store, and she also performed as a professional water-skier at the Marine World Africa amusement park south of San Francisco. Debbie has public relations running through her veins. There is a relentless pleasantness about her; she behaves as if she still has a carnation in her lapel. When she talks with her employees, "pleases" and "thank yous" are as abundant in her speech as the chocolate chips are in her cookies. They are uttered with conviction and with theatricality.

Even when she's upset with employees, and she takes her business so seriously and personally that inefficiency can "disappoint" her profoundly, she doesn't berate them. "I thought the employees were going to cry in front of me, because they wanted to do their very, very best," Debbie said of an incident that had occurred the day before when demand at one of her stores was so great they ran out of cookies. "I said, 'The most important thing is that I don't care about today. As far as I'm concerned it's history. But there's tomorrow. And tomorrow I want you to be at the winning gate. I want you to learn from today and be better for tomorrow.'"

Debbie already displayed extraordinary drive and discipline in her early teens. She saved virtually every cent she earned in high school. At sixteen, she bought herself a brand new Volkswagen Beetle.

In school she wasn't as successful. "I was never truly accepted by my peers; I don't know why," she said. "You have to understand that being in a family of five, it was very important to somehow get recognition, and the only way to get recognition was to be unique. When my friends were involved with drugs, I wasn't into it. If everyone is taking drugs, I don't want to have to do that. I want to do something different. That did not lend to my popularity. I spent a lot of time by myself, which is interesting because I love to be with people."

But it wasn't as if she was giving guys the *go* sign either. "I never liked boys my own age," she said. "I always felt we were on different wavelengths. I never dated. It was never important to me. I spent most of my time working, and I really enjoyed working." At school dances, at the senior prom, and even at the ceremony where she was crowned homecoming queen, Debbie Fields didn't have a date. "It absolutely broke my heart," she recalls. "It was one of those situations where I had to ask a gentleman out." Debbie even asked Randy to marry her.

There are at least two sides to Debbie. She says she runs her life and her company on intuition, on emotion, yet she can be as coolly calculating as a world-class poker player. She can take care of herself in any situation, yet she insists she lacks self-confidence. "I put on a great show, but I am not very self-confident," she said. "I never think that I'm great, because I know I'm not. When people say, 'God, Debbie, you are so successful,' I get uncomfortable, because I'm still striving. I know what I want and it's up there and I'm not there yet."

Debbie is sure there are things she's failed at in life, but she can't recall any off the top of her head. She's like a self-correcting typewriter that makes its errors invisible. "You can either be really depressed and give up, or you can say, 'I'm a survivor, and what I'm going to do when I make a mistake is evaluate exactly what happened and work so that it will never happen again. And I appreciate the fact that it happened so I can learn.' So it's picking up the pieces and always moving on, always, never stopping."

Debbie's stores are colorful oases that stand out in sterile, shopping-mall America. The young women in ruffled blouses and red skirts offer smiles and free cookies to customers. In this world, people who abscond with the baskets of free samples are not condemned for their greediness. "An employee will say, 'It really upsets me when one person takes the whole basket,'" Debbie explains. "I say, 'Look at it as a compliment. The fact that they were willing to walk up in front of all those customers and eat the entire basket in front of you by stuffing it in their mouths is a compliment. They love your cookies. That takes guts. They're willing to be outrageous right in front of you.'"

Debbie uses the word "outrageous" a lot to describe the way she wants her employees to behave. But in a world where the birds fly through the bubble gum trees, as the song goes, the word is defined differently than it is in Webster's. "Outrageous is a word I use a lot," Debbie said. "It means an individual is willing to do whatever it takes to make somebody smile."

If an employee sells a "baker's dozen," Debbie expects the employees to click their heels and shout "Hurray!" Since they get a commission of cookie sales in addition to salary, some do. "You've got to be willing to put yourself out," Debbie said. "It's being on stage and having fun while you're doing it."

She recalls a recent victory over the forces of grumpiness during which a customer with a chip on his shoulder, and not a chocolate one, abused her. "He was really mean to me," Debbie recalled. "I asked him, 'Have you ever had these cookies before?' and he said, 'No, I've heard about them, and I want them, so hurry up.'

"I said, 'Sir, I want you to know what you're getting if you've never had them before, so let me give you a free sample.'" Debbie's tone of voice is that of Miss Wyoming trying to convince the judges to crown her Miss America." 'I don't care,' he said, and I said, 'Sir, I'm really sorry that you're upset, but I really want to please you, and if we have to be here all day, I want you to know that you're getting exactly what you want.' So finally he took a bite of the cookie and he smiled and said, 'Thank you very much.' I hope that he learned. If anything, he learned he shouldn't handle people that way."

Clearly, Debbie has a higher purpose than simply selling a dozen cookies. "I'll be sitting up in the middle of the night thinking about the welfare programs and social security," she said. "My husband thinks I'm a nut because I'm always thinking of new systems to better the world."

Her relationship to her employees resembles that of a religious leader to her followers. "I've grown a lot through this company towards people," a store manager said. "It's people-oriented. I can see I've become more aware of people taking care of customers, their needs. The attitude comes from Debbie right on down."

"We have so many people who don't just want to be present. They want to be achievers and they give 100 percent," Debbie said. "We have people coming in Saturday's just because they want to be with the company and make it better."

At management seminars, Debbie promises employees a lot more than a paycheck. "I know some of you are timid and some of you are shy," she tells them. "But I want to give you an opportunity to break out of that. I want you to develop skills so that even if you don't stay with the company you walk away a better person."

"I want them to feel that Debbie Fields is on their side," she explains. "No matter what problems they get into, they know that if their family's not going to help them, the company will be there. Whether they need financial help or doctors or a call every day in the hospital; I will call whoever it takes to get a doctor in there three times a day and a full-time nurse."

It's hard to understand how Debbie can play Mother Theresa and still turn a profit. Certainly she has helped employees she knows personally, but it seems logistically improbable that she can provide direct care to almost a thousand people spread across a continent. Sometimes you get the feeling she's describing her vision of the world, rather than the world itself. "The company is expanding. Everyone is saying, 'It can't be done, you can't have a personal company,'" she acknowledges. "But I will create it. It is my goal. I want people to feel Debbie Fields is only a phone call away."

Debbie donates all cookies more than two hours old to the Red Cross. Through generous contributions, she has set out to cure cystic fibrosis, the number one genetic killer of children. Her attitude towards disease is as fearless and straightforward as it is towards her competition in business. She said she selected cystic fibrosis over another disease such as cancer, "because I can't cure cancer. You have to remember my philosophy. I want to be on the winning team and the doctors told me that, conservatively, we're ten years away from a cure."

Debbie adheres to the same high standards of quality with daughters Jessica and Jenessa as with her cookies. "They have lots of toys, tons of toys, but the toys I buy them are educational," Debbie said. "I justify the toys by saying it's going to teach them something. We have an Apple computer and Jessica already knows how to work it.

"I don't believe in any kind of barrier," she continues. "When Jessica was ten months old, she was walking. It's not because she's brilliant. It's because I believed she could do it."

"She's a great mother," Debbie's friend Joy Kellman said. "Her family comes first, and that's something unique with someone as successful as she. The youngest is a baby, and Debbie spends a lot of time holding her and talking to her. The older child gets a lot of educational conversation. She does not pamper the children. She's quite strict."

Debbie and Randy take the kids, and however many nursemaids are required to watch over them, on business trips. When she couldn't take the children on a recent, three-day whirlwind business trip to the Far East where she's considering opening stores, Debbie dropped them off in Hawaii and flew her parents over from California, so the kids wouldn't feel left behind.

Her relationship with Randy, both personally and professionally, is also excellent. "The most impressive thing about them as a couple is that they are incredibly synergistic; they really build on each other," Joy Kellman observed. "They have divided their cookie business into the areas that interest them. There's no overlapping. He is intellectual and she is instinctual. The sum of the two of them is greater than either one of them individually could be."

Debbie is also a community mover in Park City, Utah. The Fields own the community theatre, and are on a first name basis with the mayor and local congressmen. The cookie queen recently won an award as one of Utah's foremost business figures—no small feat in a state where the Equal Rights Amendment was laughed out of the state legislature.

She was also named one of the best-dressed women in Utah. The Fields are not Mormons. "My image there is very, very positive," she said. "I'm definitely non-threatening because I have the same value system—family first.

"One of the nice things about living in Park City is the opportunity for change," Debbie said. "We would like to see something like the Aspen Institute in Park City, to have more of an intellectual atmosphere as opposed to a ski resort."

Debbie said she'd much rather spend money on her environment than on herself. She owns little jewelry. "It's beautiful, but it's not for me," she said. "I've never had jewelry, and I think people would just be staring at the jewelry. I kind of consider myself somewhat simple."

Her California home is spacious but not lavish. There is a swimming pool and a large yard littered with toys. She is particularly proud of the kitchen ceiling she had painted to match the floor and counter tiles. The furniture also reflects her personality. The colors are strong and bold and practical. There is little around that is delicate, fragile, or frivolous.

Debbie may be a multimillionaire, but she still pinches pennies. "The carpets, I bought them at auction; I mean I stole them," she boasts. "I really have a sense of value. I love buying things as bargains. I love to negotiate. I'll negotiate with Sears. I'll call them up and say, 'Do you want to sell the TV today?' I'll tell them there's a guy down the street whose selling the same TV for less. I know it's different, but I'm really a deal person. It's the challenge of being able to buy things. Money means nothing unless you're able to have fun with it."

Saving money at Sears is a pastime. Saving money at Mrs. Fields Cookies, Inc., is a passion. "I've seen her get down and fiddle with expenses at the $10 a month level," Randy said. "There's a paradox in the spending in this company. There's almost no limit to what she'll spend on people and their development, but the wasting of a paper clip is a cardinal sin."

"The business has more financial controls than you can believe," Debbie brags. "We have P&L's [profit and loss figures] at nine the next morning for every store. I know exactly what the customer count was, what the food cost was, what the productivity was, on and on. Our controls are incredible."

Randy, the Stanford-educated whiz kid, is frankly puzzled by Debbie's success. It's not like any of the case studies from business school. "As a business person having watched this thing and having looked at a whole bunch of others, I'm now convinced that too many people focus on the making of money, because when you focus on money, it makes it easy to compromise your standards. Debbie runs the business on aphorisms and one of them is, 'Quantity follows quality.' I suppose my way of putting it as a business person is, 'Profit will take care of itself.' Maybe the most important thing to learn from Debbie is that formal education is not a prerequisite to success."

Debbie denies there may be genius lurking behind those big blue eyes and chisled cheekbones. "See, I know I'm not brilliant," she said. "I have to work. When I was in school, I really had to work. It did not come easy. My greatest strength is that I have a great deal of common sense."

"Debbie does not have education. She is not an intellectual, but she has an incredible instinctual nature," Joy Kellman said. "She can play word games, checkers, chess, and nobody can beat her. I don't care how brilliant the person is at the other end of the game, or how strategic they are, she beats them. There is no strategy game she can't win."

Randy denies that Debbie has the killer instinct, but she can subtly demolish the competition in a few words.

On Famous Amos Cookies: "I think they're very good, crunchy, packaged cookies."

On David's Cookies: "I don't see David as competition. His cookies are $6.00 a pound. Ours are $4.19."

In Debbie's game plan, the cookie stores may prove to be but the cornerstone of an empire. She plans to open a prototype chocolate store in California and will soon unveil a third store type, which she's keeping secret. A frozen cookie concoction is but the first of a dozen products that will be sold in the cookie stores and ultimately find its way onto the grocer's shelf. Bloomingdale's is also selling her cookies. Debbie said that one of her goals is to one day be as familiar in American homes as Betty Crocker.

Though many customers still assume Mrs. Fields to be a kindly old grandmother, Debbie isn't afraid to shatter their illusions by appearing on TV and in magazines. The A.M. talk shows want her recipes, and the newsmagazines want to discuss profits. She'd rather not.

When *Fortune* magazine approached her about an article, she said she tried to dissuade them. "I told them I was honored, but I don't want to be aligned with that kind of thinking," she said. "I'm not in this business to make millions. I don't want to be in the financial section. I want to be in the food section. I'm a homemaker."

Still, in the next breath, when discussing shows on which she'd like to appear, she can remark, "To kill would be Johnny Carson. Johnny Carson owns top-of-mind position."

In a consumer cosmos, the Platonic ideal of excellence is translated as "top-of-mind position." Debbie Fields is approaching that ideal fast. "I was in one of my stores a few days ago and customers were asking me for my autograph," Debbie recalled. "And I said, 'Why do you want my autograph? It has no value. Here, I'll give you a cookie instead.'"

John Davis

The film's director called John Davis at eight o'clock Saturday morning to complain about the writer. A few minutes later, the writer called to express his own reservations about the director. John Davis had been up until three in the morning reading scripts, and he'd hoped to sleep uninterrupted until eleven o'clock. Being studio executive for small movies at 20th Century-Fox may conjure up images of escorting starlets to the Oscar ceremonies, but more than anything else it's playing shrink to some of the most highstrung people in Hollywood.

"You have to realize the collaborative form of this art," John said speaking from his home later Saturday morning. "You have to be able to provide support, to be willing to listen. In a sense it requires a wise mother hen."

It's a role that comes naturally to John. He speaks of family values and the importance of friends. He says it's more important to him that he be judged honest than successful. His demeanor is placid, his light blue eyes gentle, and he cracks jokes continuously. At twenty-nine, he looks less like a power-crazed movie mogul than the relentlessly courteous assistant manager of a midwestern bank.

"He's not your average hard and hackneyed studio exec," said Lyndall Hobbs, who is directing her first film for John. "He's got a fresh approach that hasn't been spoiled by growing up in the "biz." He has lots of ideas that aren't the result of reading the *Hollywood Reporter.*"

One reason for John's refreshing attitude is that he didn't have to claw his way to the top. His father, the oil billionaire Marvin Davis, bought 20th Century Fox a couple of years ago and offered John, just out of Harvard Business School, one of the top jobs.

Much as that may sound like anybody's dream it wasn't long before John found out how hard it is to make a movie, to discover great scripts, to convince the few directors and writers of genius to work with you, to orchestrate the egos and anxiety-attacks of the hundreds of people it takes to make even a small movie. "I feel that any time anyone gets a movie to the shooting stage, they deserve a medal—it's the hardest thing in the world," John said. "It's a business fraught with disappointment." After one year on the job, John has still not started filming his first movie.

He also found out fast that the glimmering sea of show business is infested with sharks. "Some people say he got his job because of his father," explained Elizabeth Cantillion, a friend of John's in the movie business. "They make judgments before they know him. They say, 'What does he know about movies? He comes from Harvard. How dare he order us around.' I think it will be very difficult for him when his first picture comes out because he will be under a miscroscope."

If John feels the pressure, it doesn't show. "The most important thing is putting that stuff out of your head," he said. "Otherwise, you start second guessing yourself, which keeps you from making decisions."

John hasn't had any difficulty making gutsy moves. Only

days before he was to start filming, he pulled the plug on a movie he'd inherited from Sherry Lansing, the former president of Fox. "The director came in with a script that I felt made it too small a story; therefore its commercial aspects were very limited," John explained. "I figured saving $5 million was almost as good as making $5 million. Sometimes in this business people are afraid to piss off the creative community, or they're afraid of what people are going to think when they pull the plug on something. A lot of bad movies get made that way."

He currently has fifteen projects in development, and he does things his own way. On one project he persuaded the film's writer/director to become its producer, and brought in Lyndall Hobbs, who had never directed a feature film, to direct it. John was impressed with a short film he'd seen of hers. "It's slightly odd he hired me," Hobbs admitted. "I'm surprised he didn't get an experienced director. But I think that's great. It takes courage."

If John fails in Hollywood, it won't be for lack of trying. He puts in ten-hour days at the office, screens several movies a week, and says he spends as many as sixteen hours every weekend poring over scripts in search of the next *Rocky* or *Breaking Away*. "It's a very time-consuming business," he said. "It's got to be your life."

Until he accepted his offer to work at Fox, John had spent much of his life trying to prove to his father that he could be successful doing things his own way. Marvin Davis had parlayed his intuition and energy into an empire that included vast oil and real estate holdings. Scores of MBA's worked for him, though he'd never gotten or needed the degree himself. When John was accepted at Harvard Business School, a feat that would have made most parents pop open a bottle of champagne and boast to the neighbors, his father essentially shrugged his shoulders. "I don't think he understood why I really needed to go to Harvard, because he didn't need to go and he did very well," John recalled. "I had some other values. Part of it is that if I was going to be a business person I wanted the intellectual satisfaction as well as the practical satisfaction. My family was overly entrepreneurial, and Harvard had a scientific, managerial approach to things."

The road that led to John's Harvard acceptance is a Horatio Alger story in itself. In second grade, John did so poorly he was left back. Perhaps he was already suffering from living in his father's six-foot-five shadow. According to John, none of his four brothers or sisters excelled academically either. "It was devastating to me," he admitted. "You don't understand at that age that it's not intelligence, it's skill level. I've always had an academic chip on my shoulder since then."

He struggled along at a snail's pace until he was fifteen. "When I was in ninth grade, I was second from last in my class," he said. "I guess it was an attitude about myself. I didn't feel I was that bright. What happened is I hit tenth grade and I said, 'I just don't feel like feeling that way any more.' So I decided to start studying to see how well I could do. I was number one or number two in my class in tenth, eleventh, and twelfth grade."

He attended Bowdoin College in Maine where he was a James Bowdoin Scholar, and he more than held his own at Harvard. When he graduated, he had his choice of jobs. Richard Lamm, the governor of Colorado, offered John a full-time position on his staff after John spent a summer coordinating a part of the governor's oil shale policy. Davis also considered job offers from a California cable sports network, from a Wall Street brokerage house, and from the University of Denver to teach a business policy course. He and a friend even started to raise funds to finance a venture capital firm.

Coming from a family of such wealth, why did John feel the need to make more? "That was an opportunity to make my own money quickly," he explained. "If you do well in venture capital the rewards are very handsome. Of course, the thing I wanted to do was establish my own identity, mark my own place."

With that desire having sparked his drive since adolescence, his father's offer to work with him at Fox was a mixed blessing. John said he searched his soul before he took the job. "When you're trying to establish your own reputation, the toughest thing in the world is to work in your father's business," he said. "I think Freud said that your heart should take precedence over your head twice in your life, when you pick a career and when you pick a mate. So I let my heart carry me away on this one."

Marvin Davis visits the Fox lot only once every two weeks, but he speaks with John twice a day on the phone. "I facilitate his ear into the company," John said. "The older I get, the more I enjoy my relationship with him. You know you worry when your father gets older. You want to get everything out of that relationship you can. Our relationship, the older we get, gets closer and closer and closer. I like that feeling, and I don't ever want to feel I've missed out on it."

John's father is only fifty-seven, a youngster compared to other great entrepreneurs who work ten-hour days into their eighties. He tends to be overweight but is in excellent health. John's perhaps exaggerated concern underlines the central role the family plays in his life. The stability it provides has helped him remain unaffected despite the power he wields in Hollywood and the pleasures that could be his for the taking.

"I didn't grow up out here. I grew up in Colorado where there's a sense of values," he said. "Parents don't get divorced. People are fairly industrious and hardworking. I'm a product of all that. One of the things I worried about when I came to California was that I would lose some of my seriousness, some of that purposefulness in life. As it turned out, my fears were benign. But I didn't know that, what with the lights, the glamour, all that."

At times John sounds more like a Jewish grandmother than a hard-boiled studio boss. Perhaps it comes from growing up Jewish in a community where there weren't many Jews. "I'm often more comfortable around Jewish people and people from other cultures that share those values," he said. "I think there's a sense of tradition, a sense of belonging. That's very important."

Davis is extremely close to his mother; he speaks with her on the phone every day. "My Mom was always the person who told me it's most important that you be happy. It's important to blend someone who said that with someone who was subconsciously communicating, 'You've got to be very successful.'"

When he went to Harvard, John worked hard, but never

harder than he had to. He was never stricken by the competitive paranoia that consumed many of his fellow students.

"It's important that I be successful, but that I don't leave a lot of bodies behind me," he said. "The quality of life is really more important to me than the quantity of what I have. The quality of my friendships is more important than any material things I have."

Which is not to say that John lives a monastic existence. When he took the Fox job he told friends he was going to set new standards for movie moguls by renting a Ford Granada. He was joking; he bought a Ferrari. He's also not embarrassed or guilt-ridden about his wealth. When a flirtatious starlet at a party asked him if he'd ever skied Aspen, John told her he owned it. The family does.

"He really gets a kick out of it without getting carried away by it," said David Crane, one of John's oldest friends from Colorado. "His dad is the same way. If something were to befall him, he'd just go play golf. All this other stuff is enjoyable for the time it lasts."

There's also a message behind John's willingness to casually flaunt his wealth. He doesn't find it at all unfair that one man can have so much money. He sees it as testimony to the splendor of a system that allows an individual to make a billion dollars from nothing. "The capitalistic system encourages risk-takers in such a way that the entire society benefits from it," he asserted.

There may be more important things to John than making money, but he still loves doing it. Much of the father's entrepreneurial zeal has rubbed off on the son. Despite the demands of his job, he still finds a few hours a week to play the stock market and to pursue other business interests.

"Real estate financing is particularly interesting to me," he said. "I would love to get back into mergers and acquisitions and venture capital in some way. Running conglomerates is fascinating to me also."

John freely admits that though he wants to master the art of movie-making, he's not willing to spend his whole life doing it. He hopes to run all of 20th Century-Fox some day. "I became very interested in large scale organizations at Harvard," he said. "To me the fact that Fox was diversified, that they were into Aspen and Pebble Beach and Coca-Cola of the Midwest, was more interesting than the fact that they were in the movie business."

"I was born in a log cabin in Illinois," John said, leading me into his big but cozy office in the Production Bungalow on the Fox lot. "We had the only heated, log-cabin swimming pool in the neighborhood."

John's sense of humor is the butt of other people's jokes. David Crane insists that the only change that would happen to John if he lost all power and prestige is, "not as many people would laugh at his lousy jokes."

John's breakfast, a bowl of fresh strawberries, a croissant, and a cup of hot chocolate, wait for him on the coffee table. When a speck of strawberry somehow finds its way onto John's sideburn while he's devouring the fruit, I alert him to this fact. "I did it for a reason," he says without losing a beat. "It's in case I get hungry later."

At the mention of a mutual friend, John will invariably announce, "Ask her when she's going to pay me the money she owes me." or, "Oh, is she out of jail yet?"

In fact, John's jokes, which he delivers in a kind of Bob Newhart deadpan, are quite good. It's not until you get to know him better that you realize he thinks he's very funny, possibly funnier than the people he hires to write, direct, and produce his comedy films. When a journalist showed John the draft of a story he'd written about him, John had no qualms about punching it up—though the journalist never asked for John's help.

There's an autocratic streak to his personality. "He's certainly getting more involved than most executives would. I wouldn't hesitate to say he gets a little too involved," said a director who has come to expect calls from John in the wee hours of the morning. "I think once you hire people, you have to give them a certain amount of creative freedom."

However, the director added, "His sense of story is actually very good. I should say more his sense of moods and feelings. He certainly cares much more about story lines than most people. So it's a two-edged sword. There's the interference aspect, but there's the involvement aspect that is reassuring."

"I think John has very good instincts about stories, about quality, about commercialism," said Elizabeth Cantillion, who has read several of the scripts John is working on. "Fortunately for him, he didn't have to beat his way to the top, so he can remain more true to himself. He doesn't have to sell himself to anybody. In this town, people end up shelving their personal integrity because they have to bend so far to sell something."

John sold a treatment he wrote about a boy who finds a flying saucer to Interscope Communications, which is not affiliated with Fox. He has also written another treatment for a movie about a black Santa Claus, to be directed by Ron Howard and produced by Frank Capra, Senior, and Frank Capra, Junior.

John is confident of his commercial taste. He thinks he knows what the primary, American movie-going audience —people between the ages of fifteen and twenty-four who see an average of ten films a year—wants, and that he can deliver it to them. "That is a fairly sophisticated group of people," he said. "You've got to give them a reason to sit there for two hours. You can't just give them raw sex or slapstick comedy. You've got to give them a story that is compelling. I don't think you should look down on them."

The scripts John chooses to develop tend to reflect his own priorities. The small movie, because of its limited budget, focuses on people rather than hardware, on interior turmoil rather than on high-technology wars in distant galaxies. Thus, it is tailor-made to John's talents and sensitivities.

"It's a story of a hero and an apprentice hero, about a cool kid and a wimp," John said, describing the film Lyndall Hobbs is directing. "It's about adolescence and growth, about girls and being uncomfortable around them and developing a sense of confidence. It's about anger. It's about the difficulty of dealing with one's parents. It's about," John said, summing up the plot succinctly, "a guy trying to help another guy get laid."

Perhaps what John is most confident of is his worth as a human being. There is no occasion he rises to as much as helping a friend work out a problem. He would have made a great psychologist. "If you're a good person and an honest person, it will come back to you," he insisted. "You will attract the right kind of people, because a lot of them have those values also."

But what about the bastards that make it to the top? "My question is how many people are willing to do business with them? How many of them can live with themselves? How many of them would you like to be like?" Davis asks. "I look at a lot of corporate chiefs I've grown up around, and a lot of very successful politicians, and I don't find a lot of real assholes—especially in the movie business."

Davis asserts that there are no great differences among the seven largest movie companies. Over the last ten years, each has held a fairly consistent market share. All of them are competing for the same few great writers, directors, and producers. He believes what gives one studio the edge over another is the interpersonal skills of the people who run it, their ability to attract talent.

"If people feel they can get a fair break from you, that you are a person they can understand, that you won't screw them, that you care about things other than simply making money or cutting somebody else's throat, that's what in the long run will attract people to you and make you more successful," he said.

But then again, John has the time to develop relationships that other executives might not. The average life of a studio exec is eighteen months. Getting fired is a problem Davis doesn't have to worry about.

He often invites writers, directors, and producers to his beach house for small dinner parties that include his friend Bobby Shriver, the nephew of President Kennedy, Bobby's sister Maria, and her boyfriend Arnold Schwarzenegger. John also often goes to Arnold and Maria's house for dinner. He shies away from the Hollywood parties covered in the tabloids. He doesn't think his low profile hurts him in this publicity-crazy community.

"My father and I discussed this," he said. "Yes, it is important to get a certain amount of visibility, but there are parties to go to every single night of the week, and I just couldn't do that to myself. I love sitting around doing nothing. To me being able to come home from the office at seven, watch the news, and talk on the phone to friends in New

York and Boston, is more appetizing than anything else I could do.

"The lack of visibility can backfire more for other people than it can for me," he added. "Obviously, I have a certain power niche because of who I am. A lot of people will naturally seek me out."

After two years, John admits that Hollywood still intimidates him. "When I walk into a party at Sue Menger's house [the queen bee of Hollywood agents] and Jack Nicholson's there, and Michael Caine, and Ryan O'Neal and Farrah, and Sidney Lumet, and Dick Zanuck, sometimes I go to the bar and grab a drink first."

One drink is usually all it takes before he starts feeling like himself again. "I had an argument with Carroll O'Connor at the Matthaus' house two weeks after I got out here," John recalls. "You sit down and you're yelling and screaming, and you realize that this person you're yelling and screaming at is someone you've watched on TV for fifteen years—and he doesn't understand economics."

"I had T-shirts made the other day," Lyndall Hobbs said. "They said, 'Father knows best.' I crossed out the father and put 'John Davis knows best.'"

Christie Brinkley

At an age when other tots had trouble tying their own shoelaces Christie Brinkley was training herself to be special, different—a star. "As a child I walked around speaking fake French, singing fake French songs—everything was building up to my life in France," she remembers. "I was always the A student in my art class. I went to the Lycée Français de Los Angeles so that I'd be able to speak French. At eighteen I went to France, and I studied art and I lived there for three-and-a-half years. I lived in Montparnasse, of course, in a little room underneath the roof with one little window."

Her accent is *superbe,* and there are words she utters effortlessly in French for which she can't find English equivalents. If you had to point to one thing that separates Christie from the great majority of humankind, it's that while they grope awkwardly towards the ideal, she sees herself as encompassing it. Her beauty is a case in point.

She's considered a "California Girl," probably because she was born there, has blond hair, and a sun-ripened smile. On closer inspection there's nothing about her looks that can be categorized. In the way she puts herself together, the way she walks into a room, the way she uses her hands when she speaks, and in the precision of her diction, it's quite clear her role models aren't Farrah, Cheryl, or Brooke. Rather it's someone mythological, someone whose profile would be captured in the brush strokes of a Botticelli and not in the camera lens of pushy paparazzi. Just the way she had a sense of herself as an artist when she was a teenager, Brinkley has a sense of herself as a great beauty today. Though spontaneity and naturalness are her stock in trade, she is very much her own creation. Her presence is as much psychological as physical. She is startling.

"She has a very strong sense of her own stardom," said Alex Chatelain, a fashion photographer who has photographed Christie many times and is also a personal friend. "She loves it. She thrives on it. She walks through airports in ways I would never dare let anybody of my family walk through. She'll wear a bright purple leotard and high heeled shoes, and that's it. She loves that role."

Brinkley has probably been idolized in print as much as any other twenty-eight-year-old icon of eighties mass culture, so one can't blame her if some of her answers sound rehearsed. Sometimes you get the feeling she's poeticizing her personality rather than revealing it. Still, she manages to come off sensitive and approachable. She's not a snob.

"It sounds weird but she's very real," said a source in the fashion world who has worked with many models who aren't. "She has very good intentions. Her intentions are the way she looks. She's not a malicious type."

The story of Christie's start in modeling is, of course, the stuff of every adolescent female's fantasies. "I literally bumped into a photographer on the street, and he said, 'I'm looking for a girl just like you for this job and it's great money,'" Christie recalls, sounding as if she were telling the story for the first time. "Since I wasn't getting very good money as an illustrator, and I needed some, I thought, I'll do one job." This encounter occurred on a Parisian boulevard.

"I went to the modeling agency, and there were all these photographers standing around. One said, 'I'm booking her for a trip to Morocco.' Another said, 'I'm booking her for a trip to Ceylon.' 'I'm booking her for a trip to Japan.'"

She decided to go with the flow. "I was just astonished. I love to travel. So I thought, 'All right, I'll do a few jobs.' And one job led to another. The first day I went in, I did a cover for an English magazine. The second day I did a cover for a French magazine. And the third day I did French *Vogue*."

"My parents were the type who said, 'Who cares if you fail. It doesn't matter. It's the fact that you go out and try—that makes you a success.'" Brinkley insists she never thought of herself as model material before she was stopped by that photographer. "I was a bit heavier. Now I'm about 115 pounds. I was maybe 130. But I figured the worst they could say was, 'She's too fat,' or 'She's too California-looking.' I thought, Who cares. I'll just go in and try it out."

Christie is sitting in the Palm Court of the Plaza Hotel in New York eating a croissant. She says she's a slob, but not a crumb drifts onto her exquisitely orchestrated outfit: charcoal grey woolen pants and blouse, with a gossamer black-and-white mini-dress knotted around her neck like a scarf—in accord with the fashion in France at the moment. Christie also had on grey socks, and sandals bound with rubber bands. "My prerequisite for purchasing anything is that I can sit cross-legged," she said, buttering a second croissant. "This is my Chinese peasant look."

Mao Tse-Tung would probably have disagreed, but then he didn't grow up in Malibu. Christie's father is Don Brinkley, the producer of such hit TV shows as "Trapper John, M.D." and "Medical Center." According to one of Christie's attorneys, the model is but the most famous member of a family of champions. "A lot of models come from poorer backgrounds and are overwhelmed by the sudden money and fame," the lawyer said. "Christie's not. She was raised in a family where money was never the most important thing to worry about, and she's led a 'class' life all along. Her mother is a stunning beauty—California blond, slim, tan, athletic. Christie's father has always been successful. He's a brilliant writer and producer. Her brother Greg, who is two years older, also has a blond California beachboy look. He's a nutritionist. The whole family is into health and nutrition. They're all vegetarians."

"My mom's philosophy, which I heard over and over again is, 'Live every day as though it's your last,'" Christie said. "And, 'You're better than nobody and nobody's better than you.' It always sort of stuck."

Though she may believe she's no better than anybody else, she behaves as if everything she does is significant. "I have a little journal," she announced, as if the information might somehow be useful on the evening news programs. "Some days I'll write what happened during the day. Some days I'll write on just one subject. Some days it'll just be a drawing. Some days I'll just draw myself running around from this little thing to that. I always lay it out like a book."

Matisse is her favorite artist, she said, because, "his paintings are so light and pretty. The colors, the subjects, seem to show a life-style that is so happy and nice, and the colors are so pleasing."

If it seems as if the model's world is like a Matisse canvas, always intensely colorful and radiant, she disagrees. "I don't think I've had an easy life," she said. "I say I'm lucky because when something bad happens to me I think I'm able to deal with it in a pretty good way. That makes me lucky. Some people fall apart at the first little thing that happens. I've had some pretty major things happen to me."

Three weeks before this interview took place, Christie's boyfriend, Olivier Chandon, died in a racing accident. The tabloids gave the story the space usually saved for the outbreak of war. "Tragedy of the Champagne Heir and the Super Model," trumpeted the *New York Post*. "CHRISTIE BEGGED HIM TO QUIT."

In fact, the couple had broken up before the accident, but Brinkley said his death affected her deeply.

"Now I'm alone," she added, wringing her napkin. "I have to keep busy, and I want to keep busy with real quality type stuff. With a lot of people, something bad happens and they don't want to face it, so they just busy themselves and go to parties. I feel you have to face what happened and feel it and experience the pain, really face up to it. And you have to channel your feelings and emotions into something positive."

Christie is taking acting, dance, piano, Tae Kwon Do, and Italian lessons. She's also not alone. She's dating Billy Joel, the singer, who started courting her on the Caribbean island of St. Barts after she'd broken up with Chandon but before his fatal accident. "He was completely dazzled by her," said Alex Chatelain, who introduced them. "He was trying to go out with her all the time. His dream is Christie Brinkley."

After Chandon's death, Billy Joel was always there. "He was actually very, very sweet to her during that time," Chatelain said. "He'd do things like appear at her door at Easter wearing bunny ears."

In general, Christie hasn't been as lucky with men as she is with Billy Joel at the moment, according to a friend. She was married for eight years to the French illustrator and political cartoonist Jean François Allaux. She has a weakness for European jet-setters. "She's very vulnerable," the friend said. "When I say vulnerable, I mean she likes youth. She likes a certain speed of life. She's very faithful to the things she loves. She believes 100 percent in things to the point where sometimes she's totally misled."

"At times since I've gotten to know her, I feel she must really be all alone out there," Alex Chatelain said. "Only she is responsible for her success. It's not just that she's beautiful, she makes herself that way. I've been on trips with her when we'd have to shoot at five in the morning. At 3:00 A.M. she'd be up, so that she wouldn't be puffy. Nobody was asking her to do that. She has a real responsibility towards herself—that's why I feel there must be a lot of time spent alone preparing for appearances where she is really, really alone."

Some of the credit for Christie's success must go to her agents, advisors, and business associates, but it's impossible to say precisely what they have done for Brinkley that she couldn't have done on her own. Suffice it to say that she has become an industry, complete with posters, calendars, and her first book—*Christie Brinkley's Outdoor Beauty and Fitness Book*. She has also starred in her first film,

National Lampoon's Vacation, with Chevy Chase and Beverly D'Angelo.

Amid much hoopla, Russ Toggs, Inc., a clothing manufacturer, recently announced that they'd signed Christie to a contract estimated by industry analysts to be worth several million dollars. A sure sign of superstardom. The agreement calls for Brinkley to be actively involved in the design and manufacture of a line of women's sportswear that bears her name.

Christie's representatives refuse to discuss her earnings except to say she's a millionaire and that, "Christie has long since abandoned the daily work for $3,000 to $4,000 a day."

Christie's attitude towards money is casual. "I've lived with money; I've lived without money. It's no big deal for me." She's also capable of spending enormous amounts of money casually. She recently bought a duplex apartment overlooking Central Park, and friends had to do a lot of talking before finally convincing her to abandon the idea of buying what they refer to as "an incredibly expensive sailboat."

Lest it be forgotten, no matter how transcendental Christie's attitude toward the material world is, her empire was built upon a face and a body. On a recent cover of *Us* magazine, Christie was posed slipping off a skirt. A six-page spread in *People* magazine only a few weeks earlier had several photos that positively made you want to reach out and touch.

One of her agents denies there's anything exploitative about Christie's image. He insists that admiring her physique is more like saluting the flag than salivating over the centerfold in *Playboy*. "Have you seen any of Christie's calendars?" he asks. "They're not chic. They're not erotic. The photos are clean. Obviously attractive to men but she doesn't show much. The bathing suits are mostly one piece, and they're not sleazy. They're clean and wholesome, and there's nothing dirty about looking at a beautiful woman in a bathing suit."

The agent said that a Japanese firm offered Christie "what amounts to a fortune of money" to do a calendar "but we turned it down because it involved more flesh than we cared to display.

"Christie was offered a major role in a major motion picture, but they wanted one very short nude scene. She turned it down," the agent revealed. "She said, 'That's not my image, and my morals will not permit me to do it.'"

Christie is characteristically classy and also slightly evasive about the underside of the male libido. "I have to be aware of the image I project," she said, "and hope that it's a good, healthy image, because I know there are lots of young girls out there I influence."

But what about the young and not-so-young boys, those carnivorous hordes who linger by newsstands whenever Christie's picture graces the cover of a magazine? "I tried once to imagine all the people," she said. "If I walk by a newsstand and see my picture, I sort of go, 'Look, there's me.' But it's so difficult to imagine a magazine sitting on 200 million coffee tables. It's just so abstract to try and think of that.

"You realize people out there are seeing your picture when it becomes personal, when you get fan mail. I get really lovely letters. I keep expecting that pretty soon I'll start getting those bad letters. But people are wonderful. They're so nice and so sweet and just write the nicest things."

Even the construction workers building a skyscraper next door to Christie's apartment building follow *The Amy Vanderbilt Complete Book of Etiquette* when peering into her window. "Everyone thinks, 'Construction workers,' that especially with a girl like me, they would be going, 'Hey, hey, hey,' and all types of vulgar things." In fact, Christie's imitation of a sex crazed construction worker is so authentic, there is no doubt she fully understands the subject being discussed. "Even there it's 'Good Morning, Christie. And how are you today? Have a nice day.' Very friendly and nice. That's the way all my exposure comes back to me. That's the contact I have with it."

Christie's work as a photographer, and especially a boxing photographer, is considered first rate. "The best pictures that were ever done of me were done by her," Alex Chatelain said. "She has a real sense of enthusiasm mixed with her sense of humor and her joy of life. And a great eye. The camera is always there when it should be there."

Christie even has a way of transforming a boxing ring

into an idyllic landscape. "What intrigues me about boxing is that it's an individual sport where the fighters come into the ring with a personal history that will be incorporated into their fight tactics," she explained. "You can see, like with a Roberto Duran, where he comes from and his past— that he's from the ghetto, a kid that's gone hungry from Panama, and that he's going to be a real brawler. Sugar Ray Leonard is much more of a media child that's been trained very beautifully, very intelligently."

Brinkley denies the brutality of boxing. "I know all the boxers and I speak to them. To them it's not a brutal world," she argues. "Two guys are both in training. They're working for that. It's an art. Something they study for. Sometimes I do end up going, 'Ugh!' Or I'll end up in tears because I hate to see anybody get hurt. But as long as they're doing it, as long as the event's going to take place, I'll photograph it."

Though her attitudes sometimes seem over-romanticized, it's hard not to become captivated by them. "Enthusiasm is her very, very greatest quality," Alex Chatelain attested. "And when she's sad, she's almost enthusiastically sad."

Christie said she doesn't think of herself as being particularly ambitious. "Basically all I want is to be happy," she said. "I don't feel a huge, driving ambitious pressure to do anything I don't want to do."

"I've been very flexible though," she adds. "Sometimes, even though something may not be the most agreeable thing, I make a definite decision to do it because it's going to get me someplace else and will eventually make things easier for me."

Though Christie's attitude towards success appears to be nonchalant, she'll occasionally say something that reveals that she never takes her eye off the ball. Of appearing on "Tonight," the Johnny Carson show, she said, "The first time I went on the show I was so nervous because, all my life I'd think, Oh, the Johnny Carson show!"

But she claims not to lie awake at night worrying that she may be a passing fad, the celebrity model of the moment. She can sound surprisingly self-contained for a star. "When I finish a painting, it doesn't make a bit of difference to me if ten people come into the room and walk right past the painting without making a comment," she said. "I keep glancing over at it and I'm very pleased. I leave it permanently displayed, and I look over and think, That used to be a blank piece of paper, but I put those colors there. I created something out of nothing!"

"Christie loves life from day to day," one of her representatives said. "She doesn't think about what's going to be in a year or five years or ten years. That approach to life is responsible for her beauty. Christie is not a worrier.

"She's unlike anyone who has come along, perhaps ever. She has a great amount to offer the public," the agent added. "I feel that in Christie's lifetime she will gain the love of the world that Marilyn Monroe obtained—in terms of the deep, caring relationship that evolved between Monroe and the American public. I feel Christie has it in her to obtain that love."

Bryan Bantry

His teachers were surprised, and not pleasantly so, when a CBS reporter and camera crew appeared at the Browning School one morning in 1971 to interview Bryan Bantry. Browning was among the more dignified private boys' schools in New York City, and they didn't know quite how to handle a thirteen-year-old entrepreneur who was making more money than his professors, operating a dog-walking service that employed dozens of people. To make matters worse, Bryan's grades were lousy.

"The headmaster practically crucified me," Bryan recalled gleefully. "I remember getting so many report cards saying, 'Bryan's mind is somewhere else.' One teacher told me I should get out of school. That was the only encouraging word I got."

After walking several hundred more of Park Avenue's most pampered pooches, appearing on "To Tell The Truth," and being crowned Kid Capitalist by a local business magazine, Bryan took the teacher's advice. He dropped out of school at the age of sixteen and embarked on the career that has made him, a decade later, one of the more powerful and controversial figures in the world of fashion. Bryan is a *Rep,* an agent who represents the people behind the cameras— the photographers, the hairstylists, and the make-up artists who make Christie, Brooke, and Cheryl look like angels beamed down from heaven.

When Bryan came on the scene, the fashion magazines and advertising agencies were taking terrible advantage of people involved in the service aspect of the industry: paying whatever they could get away with, booking them months in advance and canceling at the last minute. Bryan changed all that, insisting on standard fees and firm bookings. For his audacity and his business acumen, Bryan attracted a stable of the most talented people in the business.

Today a top photographer like Alex Chatelain or Patrick Demarchelier, two of Bryan's fifteen clients, can earn a million dollars a year; the best hairstylists and make-up artists easily make more than a thousand dollars a day. Bryan collects 25 percent of the fee for their services— 15 percent from the person he represents and another 10 percent from whoever hired them. In a 1980 article, the *New York Times* estimated Bryan's income at $500,000 a year. But simple arithmetic makes that figure seem conservative today.

Bryan also owns three airplanes that he leases to a Long Island commuter airline as a tax shelter, has interests in several Manhattan restaurants, and is the co-producer, with Karl Allison, of *Greater Tuna* and *You Can't Take It with You,* a revival of the 1936 George S. Kaufman–Moss Hart comedy that received stunning reviews and one of the most successful plays on Broadway. "Just think," said Bryan, sounding like a little boy, "maybe we'll even be nominated for a *Tony.*"

"How was a sixteen-year-old kid able to convince me to put my life in his hands?" asks Alex Chatelain, who was Bryan's first client. "Bryan had this air about him. He really understood my work and he was respectful of it. He was so enthusiastic about what I was trying to do."

At the time Bryan met Alex, "I had all the notoriety in the world," Alex recalled. "I was in all the *Vogues,* but at the same time I was screwing myself out of the commercial work. I was telling everybody to go to hell. I had bad things happening in my family, and I owed a lot of money in taxes. I was at that point where everybody freaks out."

Bryan is a brilliant organizer and he organized Alex's life. "I'm a super secretary, that's what I am," he said. "I do everything from making dentist appointments to handholding." He recently even got a client out of jail.

"I really think he helped me pull out of my problems," Alex said. "Without Bryan I'd probably be nowhere."

Bryan works in a small apartment around the corner from Carnegie Hall. He bought an East Side co-op more than a year ago and is only now moving in. He's not as good at organizing his own life as the lives of clients and friends.

Three female assistants buzz in and out of his office, like drone bees serving their queen, while Bryan spouts off rates and schedules of his hairstylists and make-up artists and coaches his secretaries on the best way to handle self-impressed fashion editors and ad agency art directors who are on hold.

Bryan describes his office as a jail cell. The only window in the room faces an air shaft. The air conditioner rumbles away. Bryan doesn't seem to realize it's winter. There's a photograph of Brooke Shields and John Travolta taken during a first encounter Bryan arranged at Patrick Demarchelier's studio; an Irving Penn photograph of a glamorous, white-gloved woman whose face remains unseen behind a wine bottle; and a watercolor of a lifeguard daydreaming under an ocean blue sky. Still, none of these objects holds one's attention for long. Only two things really count in this room—Bryan and his telephone.

"Hi, Hi, it's Bryan," says the boy-wonder, making a point of getting to the ringing phone before any of his assistants. He claims he doesn't need to see the faces of the people he does business with because he can tell their expressions by the sound of their voices. In fact, he's never met most of the people with whom he does business on a daily basis. He believes he's created a mystique around himself, and that it's part of the reason for his success. On the phone he can be impressive and intimidating. In person he's less commanding, "The Pillsbury Doughboy dressed as a preppy," is how a former employee aptly described him. Bryan insists he's painfully shy but . . .

"It's that or nothing," he tells his caller coldly. "You've always paid the service charge and you must now. Otherwise we'll just cancel, and you'll have none of my people."

"I don't think he's afraid of anybody or anything," said the fashion editor at a major magazine. "He says what he thinks."

Recently, Bryan sent a letter to an executive at one of the nation's largest magazine publishers to inform him that because of the company's record of canceling bookings with his clients, he was initiating a policy of charging double the full fee if they canceled within one business day of the booking. "My clients are much sought after professionals, and their protection is my paramount concern," he wrote.

"He's just a crackerjack negotiator," said Melissa Ekblom, Bryan's second-in-command. "He reads people very well, and he knows how far he can drive them."

"I laugh sometimes when I listen to him talk on the phone," said Bob Felner, one of Bryan's best friends. "The other party gets their words in, but it doesn't interrupt Bryan's flow. There are built-in stalls in Bryan's conversation so that the other person can say something, but the conversation is always moving in the direction Bryan wants it to move."

Bryan finally separates himself from the phone. "When I started out in this business I was so sickeningly sweet to people, and it didn't get me anywhere," he recalls. "I didn't get work for the longest time. One day I went into a meeting, and I told somebody to go screw themselves. I figured, 'Well, that's the end of that.' But the next week they called me up and gave me the job. From that day forward, I learned the hard way, you have to walk over certain people to make them respect you."

Bryan's attitude hasn't made him a lot of friends. "He's the worst," stated one editor. "People like him should not be given publicity. He's just so unpleasant and so rude and he messes everyone around all the time. The people who work with him are always apologizing, saying, 'You must believe it's not me that's behaving this way, it's Bryan.' I think he takes pleasure in it too. I think he gets off on screaming at people."

"Some people really like me and an awful lot of them really hate me," Bryan said boldly. "I'm a ball-buster at times."

Two of the people who like and admire Bryan today despised him at first. "He tried to push one of his people off on me and I didn't like the way he did it," recalled Kezia Keeble, who was a magazine editor at the time. "He did it with tone. He had an attitude."

Teri Shields, the mother of Brooke Shields, told Patrick Demarchelier, who is Brooke's favorite photographer, to punt Bryan as his agent. "I told Patrick I thought Bryan was a colossal pain-in-the-ass," she said. "I thought he was terribly rude and a snob. I'm sure Bryan's made a lot of enemies for no good reason."

But Bryan pursued friendships with both women. "He's brilliant. He has common sense," Teri Shields explained. "I hear his brain when I'm talking to him by the next question he asks. He's analyzing and trying to figure out his next step to success every second that goes by."

"He was never my rep but we had this chemistry," said Kezia. Bryan helped her establish a free-lance career as one of the top stylists (the person who selects the clothes models wear in photographs) in the business. "We appreciate one another's energy about making money and finding that a creative thing to do. We share the same fantasies about our lives and our futures. In other words, the bigness of it. If you talk to some people like that, they think you're totally bananas. But if you talk to Bryan like that, he just gets more excited."

Whether they like him or not, the fashion industry is forced to deal with Bryan because he represents so much top talent; a few clients even seem to have been created by Bryan, as if by a latter-day Dr. Frankenstein. "This twenty-six-year-old is responsible for the lives of these people who are like free-floaters in the universe but who have talent," said Kezia. "So many of them have told me they were broke until they went with Bryan; then they started making money hand over fist."

Though Bryan has no discernible taste of his own, he instinctively appreciates what other people consider to be
good taste. His Christmas card comes from Cartier. The
portfolios he assembles to showcase his clients' work are
stunning displays of salesmanship. "What we have created
here is an image for each and every one," Bryan said, leafing
through one of the books. "The mere fact that they're with
me means they're the top. I have kept a couple of people at
bay for two or three years because it wasn't time yet.

"I charge as much as I can get," continued Bryan in that
condescending singsong that has turned so many people
off. "I get as much as anyone will pay. I raise rates at the
drop of a hat. There is no rhyme or reason to how we do
things here. It's all on instinct."

Bryan denies this story, but Calvin Klein reportedly
wanted one of Bryan's make-up people to work on a commercial. The person was already booked by another client.
The fee Bryan demanded to take her off that job was so outrageous that Klein vowed never to use any of Bryan's people
again. He broke his promise.

"Calvin was having supper with the people who had
worked on the shooting," said a reliable source. "And he
announced to everyone there, 'I would never work with
Bryan Bantry.' And two of Bryan's people were sitting right
there next to him. One was the hairstylist and the other was
the make-up artist. And he hires these people all the time."

"When I was little I was a child model because my mother
was a model," said Bryan in a rare reference to his family.
"My father was in the film business, and later on my mother
lived with a fashion photographer who was really big in the
sixties."

Bryan has not spoken with his mother, who was a successful model in the fifties and sixties, in ten years. Within
the last couple of years, he saw her walking down Fifth Avenue and crossed the street to avoid her. "He doesn't block
her out; he just has no feeling for her," said Bob Felner.
"She was just much happier without him so he recipro-
cated."

Kezia Keeble was Bryan's confidante for two years before

she discovered who his mother was, and she did so then only because her husband asked Bryan point-blank. "My impression is that she was beautiful and living with an artist, that kind of person," Keeble said.

Not having emotional support from his family has made Bryan supremely self-sufficient. "He's very strong," Bob Felner observed. "He can make himself do things he doesn't want to do. He's not a Pollyanna. He faces reality head-on all the time. He has a very positive self-image. There's no fuzziness. There's very little posing."

"In the earlier years, people would say I was lying about my age," Bryan explained. "That was a hoot. There's a great deal of jealousy in any business. But I really don't feel as if there's a whole lot of competition. Every now and then I hear someone say that they want to be an agent like Bryan Bantry, and I think it's stupid. I feel everyone does it in his or her own way."

Bryan considers only two people, Bob and Melissa, to be his close friends; actually, they function as his family. Melissa has a couple of kids of her own, but she still finds time to mother Bryan. "She's soft and gentle and she's a ballbuster at the same time," said Bryan. "You can't walk over her. She's the only one here who screams at me and I listen . . . sort of."

"The people I've known, I've known for years and years," he added. "Everybody else I'm wary of, and if they try to get close it's practically impossible."

"Loyalty is the most important thing to Bryan," Melissa said. "If you're loyal to him, he'll be loyal to you forever, no matter what you need, whenever you need it. But if you cross Bryan, he can be very, very dangerous. He knows everybody in this business. He can call them and convince them to use a hairdresser they've never heard of before on a million dollar advertising account, because people respect Bryan's judgment. On the other hand he can prevent you from working."

Even people like Alex Chatelain, whom Bryan has represented for a decade, don't feel as if they really know him. "I don't feel like he's a personal friend," the photographer said. "Even though he's incredibly faithful to me as I am to him. He always maintains a certain distance. Once I told him something bad I'd done, and he said, 'I hate to hear that. I always imagine you to be perfect.'"

"I don't know the people I represent very well at all," Bryan admitted. "I avoid them like the plague. I mean I absolutely avoid them, because I have my own incredible little fantasy of how great they are, and I don't want to know any differently."

"There are days, especially in the winter, when I don't go out," he continued. "I really don't want to know what the real world is like sometimes. For the most part if you get to know people too well, you don't like them. I find that over and over again. A fortune teller once told me I should stop closing myself off from people, and I said, 'Okay, I'll do it.' But I realized there are so many jerks out there, and I'd rather have my fantasy of them. I do create my own world. Most people have selective hearing. I have selective world."

Bryan's most elaborate fantasy is to become a "big-time" movie producer. "I just see myself making nonstop comedies, I mean quality movies, good movies," Bryan said in his little boy voice. "I can very easily see the front page ad for my first movie. I see Oscars, I definitely do. I want them, not so much for the Oscar itself but because it will represent that I've arrived. Nothing in my life has been or will be Grade B."

Nothing is more important to Bryan than recognition. "When I go to a party I don't want to go in as a nobody," he said. "I want to go in as someone to whom people cater a little bit, because I do a lot of catering. I'm delighted when I go to these parties to have people say, "Oh, you're Bryan Bantry.' It's neat but, god, I hope I don't meet all of them, so there'll still be somebody left who will say that."

But when Bryan receives recognition it only seems to reinforce his most negative notions about human nature. Other people's reactions to the 1980 *New York Times* article about Bryan taught him something he'd already suspected. "When the *New York Times* article came out, I got a call from the head of a cosmetics company, the same person who would not return my calls a week earlier," he remembered. "I struggled in this business for years, and the *Times* came out, and overnight I was recognized. I think that's really disgusting, and hurtful—that one day I was just a jerk and the next day they talked to me. And all along, all I was trying to do was get them to talk to me." [His detractors say he is obsessed with making money. But money is most important to Bryan as a symbol of success. "Money is absolutely amazing. I think it's disgusting, and once you realize how disgusting it is, you can use it," he said.]

In the *Times* article Bryan mentioned his movie producing dreams, and the next day scripts started to pile up on his doorstep. One of them was a comedy about a tiny town in Texas called Tuna. "I just laughed and laughed and laughed, and that was it," Bryan recalled. "The oddest thing about it is that I let a lot of people read it and they didn't think it was funny at all."

But as always, Bryan followed his own gut instincts. So did virtually all his hair and make-up people. Together they invested in the show. The *New York Times* theatre critic panned it, but once again it was Bryan who has his finger on the public's pulse. The play was a hit, and Norman Lear will be adapting it for television.

"Everything is building," Bryan said ominously. "It's like this rolling stone gaining momentum. And that's scary. So much is happening ever since *Greater Tuna*. More and more scripts, more and more deals, meeting more and more people."

When the opportunity arose to co-produce *You Can't Take It with You*, Bryan jumped at the chance, calling everyone he knew and raising his share of the $550,000 it took to bring the play to Broadway almost instantaneously. The reviews the play received were so stunning that Jason Robards, the show's star, redecorated his dressing room after reading them and signed a five-month contract. Bryan and co-producers Ken Marsolais and Karl Allison are already organizing two national touring companies of the show, and Bryan is considering offers to produce a multimillion dollar musical on Broadway as well as another Off-Broadway show starring "a name actress."

Bryan doesn't rest. After working twelve to fourteen hours a day as a rep, he'll go to bed with a stack of scripts. He is also the personality editor for Italian and French *Harper's Bazaar* and for Italian *Cosmopolitan*. "I don't even get paid for that," he said. "It's a way of learning more about film people."

"I don't see how he can be happy," said a client of Bryan's.

"He has no time. Anything he does is always to get this or to do that. I've never seen him enjoy a meal. It's always a meal with somebody because this person's going to help him do this."

Bryan visits astrologers, psychics, palmists, and mind readers, but, as Bob Felner points out, it's not that Bryan's particularly superstitious. "He's always wanting to know what happens next," Bob said. "It's more caution than superstition. He's a terrible worrier, frighteningly so. He's really on a path to succeed and he doesn't want to be sidetracked."

Some people perform good deeds hoping they'll be sent to heaven. Bryan isn't prepared to wait that long. "I've helped as many people as I can, and I hope that somehow it will come back to me in my next venture," he said. "I do this really honestly. If you do everything in an honest way it will come back to you. God, I hope it starts. I think it will come back to me because I have always been in a position to give people work. I really do believe I've been put here to create jobs."

"I don't think it's a totally egocentric thing. He may make money, but he's also made money for a lot of people and he deserves every dime he gets because of it," Kezia Keeble said. "He has shown people how to open their own scope about themselves. He's always had this totally open vision, and money is only a representation of how big it is."

Perhaps the most powerful testament to Bryan's drive is that he's forced himself to become a social butterfly of late, even though making small talk with the other insects is one of the things he likes least. He knows he'll never achieve his movie-making dreams over a telephone. He must be seen by the right people, with the right people, at the right places.

Bryan attended Diana Vreeland's gala for the Metropolitan Museum's Costume Institute, *the* event of the New York social season. He was one of the sponsors of the Lincoln Center Film Society's star-studded benefit to honor Sir Laurence Olivier. When *Greater Tuna* opened at the Circle in the Square theatre in Greenwich Village, Bryan sent complimentary tickets to everyone from the teacher at Browning who suggested he drop out of school to the late actress Joan Hackett. Hackett was a friend of Bryan's mother but he hadn't seen her in several years.

"She's the one who called Norman Lear. She was so supportive, and introduced me to so many people," he said. "She was a help to me in so many other areas. It's just so weird. I was up at Elaine's [a Manhattan restaurant and celebrity hangout] with her, and all these people I'd met a zillion times before were reintroduced by her, and I existed."

If Bryan were ever to relax, one would think it would be at his summer home on Long Island. But Bryan seems as obsessed with controlling the weeds in his garden as he is about controlling his future. "It's an unpressured world, but he makes it pressured by wondering about the rabbits, and whether the asparagus is going to come up," said Bob Felner.

The only place Bryan seems to lose himself is at the supermarket. "He's totally transported," Bob reported. "He likes economy-sized things, and he's always arranging his kitchen shelves to look like supermarket shelves. He's always rearranging them to make sure they look good."

On Friday mornings in the summer, a naturalist arrives at the house to take Bryan on a nature walk. "It's hysterically funny watching him tramp off into the woods in boots looking at weeds and eating wild berries," Bob said. "Sometimes I wake up at 5:30 A.M., look out the window, and there's Bryan sitting in a rowboat on the pond straining the water, looking for the little things he's learned about. He has a terrible will to succeed, like Scarlett O'Hara. I think he's fairly lonely because of it."

Baron Jones

Baron Jones, a black man who grew up poor in Los Angeles, felt as if he'd landed on another planet when he walked into Princeton University's Cannon Club during his freshman year. "I saw this woman hanging from a chandelier with very little on, and there were guys spraying beer all over the floor," he remembers. "There were other guys reading the *Wall Street Journal* in the reading room. I wondered how all this could go on in one place."

Many of Baron's black classmates went into culture shock after similar experiences. They couldn't adjust to a way of life that seemed lifted from an F. Scott Fitzgerald novel. According to Baron, 30 percent of them dropped out in his freshman year.

Others became "Oreo cookies." To fit in they adopted the customs of their upper-crust, white classmates—the clothes, the cars, the walk, the talk. And in the process they lost their own identities. Baron didn't. He exhibited the qualities that have marked his success in everything he's done—a powerful sense of his own style, grace, and importance, and bulldog determination. He stuck Princeton out for four, often lonely years, until he got what he came for— that piece of parchment that would open doors in the white world.

"The most important thing you have to remember is that I didn't want to be white," he said. "I've always been pro-black because I've seen situations growing up and in college where black people insulated themselves from the masses of black folks who sincerely needed their help and expertise. I was determined never to do that. A large part of that was due to my mother's influence. She said, 'Never, ever forget the bridges that carried you where you're going.' And I don't ever plan to do that."

Jones is as good as his word. Last year, at the age of twenty-nine, he donated $100,000 to Princeton and to the Wharton School of Business, from which he was graduated with an MBA, to establish a perpetual scholarship in his own name for black students. What makes the gift poignant is that Jones earned his money in Los Angeles real estate— a repository of old white money and racial prejudice.

Jones's specialty is assembling parcels of land in downtown L.A. for multinational corporations. "What I'm looking for is an international reputation as a broker, and I'm starting to get that now," Baron said sipping champagne over brunch at a cafe off Santa Monica Boulevard. "I'm working heavily with the Chinese, the Arabs, and with the Europeans who, for political reasons, are moving big dollars to the L.A. area."

The art of commercial real estate consists of creating opportunities for development where none existed before. Baron Jones is perhaps better at it than any other broker in the city. "I saw an opportunity for growth that no one else saw in a certain area of downtown L.A., so let's just say I guessed right," he says with a smile.

It took a lot more than a lucky guess. The deal that established Baron's reputation was one in which he assembled a square block that was occupied by deteriorating hotels, apartment houses, vacant lots, and a church, and sold it to Manufacturer's Life Insurance Company of Canada, which plans to erect a skyscraper on the site. The strategies for putting together a deal of that magnitude are Byzantine, because the broker must negotiate with each landowner on the block separately, hoping that none discovers he's buying up the entire block for a company with millions of dollars at its disposal. If one does, he might hold out for a king's ransom and jeopardize the entire deal.

It's not unlike playing chess on a grand scale. Baron is the Bobby Fischer of the sport. "There's a combination of patience, persistence, and instinct involved," said Bruce Koerner, an architect and urban planner who has teamed up with Baron on several projects. "He has structured transactions that have been pioneer transactions—he has put together unusual syndications of people to make something happen. It's very much the case of being a master strategist.

"It's not the mere buying and selling of real estate, which many people do quite well," he added. "The factor that makes him especially strong and important is that he understands development. He reads what's going to happen in three years when others are talking about what's happening tomorrow. The bottom line result is that he has done something in moving a city forward in a very dramatic way."

Baron didn't earn a cent the first eighteen months he worked at Cushman-Wakefield, the real estate firm with which he's affiliated. Agents don't earn a salary. All their income comes from commissions. "It's a terrible thing to go through, particularly if you come from a family that does not have the resources that will allow you to continue until you make your first dollar," Baron said. "Think how it is to go for eighteen months without making money, with the wife totally supporting you. She's looking at you every day because you're supposed to be the breadwinner, and you haven't brought in a dime."

By the time he got his first break, Baron was so desperate that his clients were able to screw him out of his commission. "I was working on a major office building, and I was hungry," he recalls. "I was desperate and it showed in my face, and when that happens, the buyer or seller picks it up. The building was worth $12 million. Today, I would make $360,000 to $480,000 commission. In fact, I made a little more than $10,000. They told me, 'If you don't like it, sue us.' I was not in a position to sue them."

The experience taught Baron a bitter lesson. "It will never happen again," he vows. "From that point on, I realized that whether you have it or not, you walk in like you're worth a million dollars."

Jones looks like he stepped out of the pages of *Gentleman's Quarterly.* "My dress is Brooks Brothers with a European flair," he said. "My trademark, if you will, is that I wear a lot of double-breasted suits. I'm trying to look presentable and nice, but at the same time have my own style. I don't believe a client wants to see three Xerox types or three IBM types walk in a room. You can be successful in this business without being a conformist."

He drives a BMW 633. "In my business you need an image car," he explained. "It's black, conservative. I wanted that car since Wharton, and I promised my wife I'd never buy a car until I could buy that car. It fits with my all-or-nothing personality."

If Baron sounds like a single-combat warrior in a tailored suit of armor, that's because he is. The Los Angeles real estate establishment is composed of white blue bloods who belong to the same country clubs, summer at the same resorts, and pass their land from generation to generation. Occasionally, one of them who has spoken with Baron only on the phone and doesn't know he's black will invite him to a club where the only blacks that usually set foot inside are the waiters.

"We've always found a way that doesn't embarrass either party to work a situation like that out," said Paul Alanais, a real estate attorney and business associate of Baron's. "What we do is say, 'Why don't we take you to lunch.' Baron is realistic about the fact that there are a number of prejudiced people out there who just won't deal with him. But he doesn't take the attitude of, 'They're prejudiced so let's forget the deal.' He's a strategist. Even though he may resent the prejudice, he won't be stopped from accomplishing his objectives."

The lawyer believes that Baron sometimes tries to over-compensate for his color. "He doesn't want anybody to feel, 'Oh gee, isn't he a successful black broker.' He just wants to be the best broker in downtown. Period. He's almost compulsive in terms of success."

Baron doesn't behave compulsively. There's a sense of perfect control about him, a feeling of physical and psychological power. His voice is calm and deep, and his physique is still that of a college halfback.

He also has outlets for the pressure. He skis regularly in California and Utah, and travels to Palm Springs on weekends. "In terms of life-style, I'm one of those guys who likes to party with the next one," he said. "I probably do it more than most people, but when it comes time to hit the road on Monday morning, I'm gone."

"Baron has a quiet confidence you seldom see in people in the real estate field," Bruce Koerner observed. "Real estate people are hyperactive by nature. They're refined versions of used car salesmen. With Baron you never have the feeling you're sitting there with a real estate broker. You're sitting there with a professional man who deals in the assembly of real estate. It's a whole different thing and that's what separates him."

Baron's father was killed in a car crash when Baron was eight years old. His mother supported him and his six younger brothers and sisters until Baron was thirteen. At that time, she developed an arthritic condition and could no longer work. "It was incumbent upon us to go out and survive," he said.

Each morning before school the boys wrapped newspapers and were driven along their paper routes by a family friend. That was the closest Baron got to an entrepreneurial venture at a young age. His mother encouraged him to concentrate exclusively on his school work. When he didn't get straight A's, "She used to beat the hell out of me," Baron recalled with some satisfaction. "She always had high hopes for me and she pushed." Baron graduated second in a class of 850 students.

At Princeton he was premed, but he really majored in football, where he played halfback for the Tigers, and was a partner in a concession that sold banners and T-shirts at games. His life's ambition was to become a doctor, but he changed his mind during his senior year. What he really wanted to do was make money. He'd seen firsthand the independence it gave his rich classmates. "I truly believe, again this is the upbringing from my mother, that if I'm after money, I'll do it in business," he said. "I won't feel guilty about making money off people the way I might as a doctor."

He always felt like an outsider at Princeton. "I can recall a number of instances where I thought I was going to leave. What the hell am I doing here? I can go somewhere else and get an education at a lot less expense to myself."

When armies of Princeton men boarded buses bound for Vassar, Smith and Bryn Mawr on weekends, Baron stayed closer to home, hanging out at schools like Ryder and Manhattanville College where the social pressure was less intense. He met his wife-to-be, who went to Trenton State College, when she attended a Princeton mixer. They were married in either 1975 or 1976. "I don't remember things like that," Baron said. "That's probably why we're not together right now. She always thought there was an over-concentration on my part with regards to business."

They are separated but in the process of getting back together. "One of the things I'll do is go after a deal no matter what time of day or night, because when it hits me I want to move on it then," Baron said, explaining the roots of their incompatability. "Imagine lying there at twelve o'clock. All of a sudden an idea hits you, and you have to get to somebody right away. You get on the phone, and your wife is lying there trying to sleep. It just doesn't work out at all."

He said he roamed for a while, but he wants her back. She's his samurai mate. "There's no tougher cookie out there," he said. "I take lessons from her."

After graduating Wharton, Baron took a job as a financial analyst with TWA, but he got restless fast. "Needless to say it was not my cup of tea," he explained. "You spend years of your life working your way up the corporate ladder, and if you're lucky you'll make forty grand. For me it's all or nothing, and it's been that way a large part of my life. I think the problem with many people is they never realized that it's all or nothing, so they don't have the motivation to go out and truly succeed."

In one way, real estate may have been the perfect career for a black man determined to control his own fate. There are no affirmative-action policies. If someone succeeds, he does it on his own. It's all or nothing. When Baron discusses how effectively he works with white people who wouldn't invite him into their homes socially, his voice takes on a strange thrill. "There are guys at work who are the closest thing to John Birchers you can get, but we have a mutual respect for one another," he said. "The respect hinges on performance. If you outperform your counterpart, there's nothing a guy can do, no matter how jealous he may feel. He knows you're a competitor.

"I've got a lot of guys, and we work well together," he continues. "We all have our different styles, but when we hit a client, we hit him hard. It would amaze you. It doesn't matter what our differences are, when we hit that marketplace, we're all Cushman-Wakefield. The name of the game is we have to make the deal. That's the part of the business I like—when you see two guys who really don't like each other on the same deal, and they work like a well-oiled machine."

A year ago Baron read *A Book of Five Rings*, which marked what he describes as "a turning point in my life." Written four hundred years ago by a samurai master, the book describes the battle strategies of the samurai. "His thesis is that most samurai use two hands to fight with their swords," Baron explained. "He developed a technique where he was able to use two swords at one time and use each hand equally well. There was no way you could defend yourself against a two-pronged attack. Essentially you use the same strategies in business."

"I think Baron would have made a very good general," Paul Alanais said. "He's very perceptive about how something can come together. It really is tactics; like a general orchestrating a battle."

The Manufacturer's Life deal was a perfect arena for Baron's Patton-like skills. Over a six month period, he quietly assembled all the property on the block. "The last piece we got was owned by a very successful Chinese investor who would have been the type to hold out," Paul Alanais recalled. "But he owned a lot of property adjacent to it and Baron was able to convince him that he'd be an idiot, that he'd be slitting his own throat by holding out. His other property is now worth $10 to $15 million more than before the deal came through."

Property on the block sold for $40 a square foot before Baron discovered it. By the time he had tied a ribbon around the whole package, he had boosted its value to $230 a square foot.

He is currently putting together a deal that will dwarf all the others. On behalf of several multinational firms, he is assembling several square blocks of downtown, which, when developed, will dramatically alter the skyline of Los Angeles. The city has often been described as a suburb in search of a city. Baron Jones is helping it find itself. "To be able to assemble that much land quietly and competently and to see the future in this grand evolution—that is where he stands out from all the rest," Bruce Koerner said. "He has created a modus operandi that has not been duplicated."

Unlike other brokers whose usefulness ends when the deed is turned over to the client, Baron often remains on the project as a consultant expediting the development process through a coterie of planners, politicians, architects, and engineers. He said he expects to earn $1 million this year and to do "much better" next year. Though he entertains lavishly—at lunch he can be found in the finest French restaurants softening up power-brokers with fine food and hundred-dollar-a-bottle Bordeaux—he spends little money on himself. "I don't do anything with my money but invest in business opportunities and real estate," he said.

"I'm really on the cutting edge of what I believe is the new frontier in real estate—multi-deal brokerage," he added. "The average broker can handle only one or two deals at a time. If I'm working on ten deals and I can get seven or eight of those, I can do $4 or $5 million a year easy."

Baron has a samurai's strategy towards racism. "You have to take a two-sworded approach," he said. "You have to try to live with the system as it is but try to build a new generation of black kids to get us out of this mess."

That was the rationale behind his gift to Princeton and

Wharton. "The most important thing I would like black people in this country to understand is that no matter how bad you're doing, if you try to make sure your kids do something about it and if you do something for them to make them want to do something, it will take two generations, thirty or forty years, and we'll be out of this mess."

Baron recalls the plight of a black politician who "got busted for trivial things. It never would have happened if he had surrounded himself with people of the same ethnic group. By getting rid of him they would have known that another black person would have stepped in his place."

But Baron said the politician made the fatal error most black politicians make—he surrounded himself with white lieutenants. "By getting rid of him, they were able to get someone white who would take care of their needs. Most successful black people think the only way they can be successful is to surround themselves with white people.

"There's no infrastructure," he continued. "If a wealthy black person in this country goes down the tubes, he's got no one to rely on, because there are no black people in place to help him from getting submerged. It's not enough to have isolated examples like myself. Malcolm X said no matter how bright you are or how successful you are, if there's turmoil in this country and they start to call you 'nigger,' they don't know that you're rich or you're poor. To them you're all going to be 'niggers.'"

Baron admits his gift to Princeton and Wharton was not completely altruistic. He was doing some bragging. "For a black person to donate $100,000, it's a little different from what they anticipated when they let some of us in to fill their quotas," he said. "I was told that a lot of people at the highest levels of Wharton management were totally shocked that any black person had done it."

Even though he shunned publicity over the gift because, he said, "when you're building your career you don't want to put roadblocks out there where guys are constantly trying to chop you down," he didn't escape the attention of the black political establishment.

"I met Tom Bradley two weeks ago, and it was the first time he knew who I was," Baron said, referring to the black mayor of Los Angeles. "I'm starting to go with a group who are heavily into political circles. I've had people make the suggestion to me that I run for an Assembly seat and then maybe the State Senate. I'm not ready for it yet. I don't want anyone buying me, and I don't want to be in a position where I can be bought. The best way to do it is Kennedy style, if you will. Have it before you get there."

Lately, he said, he seems to be attending a political fund raiser every night. "It's kind of like going to Princeton," he observed. "You're in an unknown environment and you have to acclimate yourself as quickly as you can."

Jean Yates

Oriental art and the computer industry are but two of the targets of Jean Yates's soaring intellect. "You can look at it as the struggle of life against the elements," she said, referring not to Silicon Valley, where she owns a market research firm, but to a nineteenth century Oriental watercolor of a windswept bamboo that hangs in New York's Metropolitican Museum of Art.

"But when you get closer to it you just start loving the brush strokes. There's an abstract symmetry that transcends any particular statement about reality. But just the beauty of the sheer brush strokes is so . . . oomph!" "Oomph," is a sound Jean emits with relative frequency when her intellect and emotions meet head on.

"Just as I like the levels of reality you see in Oriental art, so I like the levels of reality you see in market research," she continues. "On one level you can say, Isn't that an interesting microprocessor. Then you say to yourself, How can I combine the processor into a computer with other chips? Then you ask yourself, How can I take the way the chip is evolving and change the way the computer actually acts?"

From there Jean moves onto software, networking software, packaging the product, documentation, information, and end users. The computer illiterate trying to keep up with her train of thought feels as if he's being dragged behind a horse.

"When you take all these levels of reality and start looking at the relationship between the microprocessor and the end user, it's very similar to Oriental art. My mind sees layers, within layers, within layers," she concludes, sounding more like a fortune-teller than one of the computer industry's hottest analysts.

Some would argue that in an industry where companies shoot up as fast as crabgrass, college dropouts become millionaires overnight, and revolutionary ideas become dated in a single season, any analyst is as much soothsayer as seer. Be that as it may, many people believe that twenty-nine-year-old Jean Yates sees a lot more in her crystal ball than others do in theirs. Started ten months ago with an initial investment of only $1,500, Yates Ventures publishes a market newsletter, performs research studies, and produces instruction manuals for software. Jean said she's building the company in order to sell it. Her goal is to make $20 million by the end of the decade. Interest in the company already exists, and it's conceivable she'll achieve her goal well before that.

What draws the attention of investors to Yates Ventures is the woman who owns it. She's hard to miss. At five-foot-ten and two hundred pounds, Jean is one of the stars of the computer convention circuit, an industry evangelist who tells the technomasses what's hot and what's not in a North Carolina drawl that ranges from coy to commandeering. She's a fearless prognosticator who is regularly quoted in the *Wall Street Journal, Newsweek,* and a score of industry publications.

"I'm considered a colorful person in the industry, sort of a cross between Rona Barrett and Dan Rather," she said. "I create controversy, but I back it up with market research that substantiates my point.

"I've always been someone who stood back and looked at the big picture," she added. Once Jean starts talking there's not much to do but sit back and relax. "People have always valued my ability to see and get past the marketing hyperbole. I will say: What this company is doing is stupid, these people are caught up in old mentalities, they don't understand where the market is heading. And I call them on it, and risk offending by being honest. But then I show them how to strategize successfully, so the net effect is positive."

Whether they believe her predictions or not, everybody listens. "There's too much information," explained an industry journalist, waiting in line to have a word with Jean at a convention. "In this industry, because of the chaos, you're grateful to have a high priest come along and sort it out for you. If you can get her on your side she can assure your success."

As recently as five years ago, Jean Yates knew nothing about computers. Her roommate brought home an Apple II, and on New Year's Eve 1979, Jean underwent the information age's equivalent of a religious experience. "This is like the first automobile, I said to myself. It immediately became apparent to me that this is the wave of the future," she recalled. "As a student of history, as somebody who has read a lot of books, I saw that whenever there was a major shift in an economy, the people who were in the right place at the right time were able to make out like bandits. I said to myself, 'There's never going to be an opportunity like this again in the global sense. This is an unparalleled change. The whole economy is moving from an industrial to an informational society. And I don't think it's too late to get aboard with the learning curve I have.'"

By "learning curve" Jean means intelligence, and by any measure of intelligence, she is a genius. When she was five years old her teachers thought she'd cheated on an I.Q. test because she received a perfect score. They called in her parents and they kept retesting her. "It made me feel like a freak," she said. Her I.Q. was measured at 179.

Those feelings of alienation from the provincial North

Carolina environment where she was raised only intensified as she grew into an adolescent with fledgling feminist yearnings. "When I was twelve years old, I wanted so bad to be the first woman on Mars," she recalls. "That was my goal in life. I didn't care about being the first person. But I wanted to be the first woman."

She was only following the example of a mother who went back to school and got a Master's degree in psychology after her kids grew up, and a grandmother who taught herself the law and won a legal battle over her husband's estate when he left no will. "One of the first books we're putting out is the business guide, and I'm dedicating it to my mother and grandmother, previous generations of powerful women whom I learned a lot from," Jean said.

At the same time Jean started Yates Ventures, it was discovered that her mother had a very serious illness. It's hard to tell how deeply it has affected Jean. She offers the information without comment except to say, "It's a drag," and then moves on to the next thing, like a newswire chattering information. It's not as if she seems in any way callous, only that ideas flow from her so quickly, she doesn't have time to brood.

She says she reads dozens of press releases and eighty magazines a month, in addition to the four books unrelated to the computer industry that she speed-reads every week. Recently she was plowing through a Robert Ludlum thriller, a history of everyday life during the Renaissance, a physics text, and a monograph on a private collection of European paintings. "I feel like an optical memory system," she explains. "If you ask me what I know about three-inch floppies, I could probably walk to five different places and pull the articles. I tend to absorb a lot of data really quickly. Believe it or not, when I sleep it chugs around and I'll wake up at five in the morning and say, Wow, so that's the way it's going to fall out!

"I've always had an analytic mind. I could always follow the chess game five maneuvers ahead and see what was going to happen. All any fast-moving market is, is a really big chess game on a billion dollar scale."

As someone addicted to information, Jean suffered severe withdrawal at Quail Hollow Junior High School. "My whole life from the age of twelve to seventeen was boredom," she remembers. "I was in this rural North Carolina high school where they were teaching all the girls to be housewives and all the guys to be insurance salesmen. The whole reality was that you were a football player, or a cheerleader, or an outcast."

Jean was a hippie at fourteen. At fifteen, she ran away to Woodstock. "I was looking at people my own age and they were picking which set of rules they wanted to follow, the insurance salesman rules, or the secretary rules, or the refrigerator repairman rules. And I didn't like any of these sets of rules. Basically what they were doing was shutting off their brains, and I'll be damned if I'm going to do that."

To occupy herself, Jean worked on the local underground newspaper, *Inquisition*, which published bad poetry, much of it directed at the high school principal. When he caught Jean trying to sell the rag on campus, he let her know who the "Grand Inquisitor" really was. "He belonged in a military academy," said Jean in her inimitable way of delivering bias as if it were fact. "He pulled out his notebook and read me the riot act. 'You can't sell anything on campus.' So I said, 'Fine, I'll give it away.' He was livid with rage. He just made my life miserable from that point on. I didn't care."

Jean didn't exactly send him daisies or candygrams either. "We went and dug up a pot plant we'd grown in the woods and replanted it on the front lawn of the high school," she remembers. "The plant stayed there for an entire year. It was about twenty-five feet tall. We used to go out there, pick leaves, and smoke them on the smoking patio. Finally someone told him what it was. He was just obsessed from then on to find out who did it. He never did."

He probably had a pretty good idea. When Jean applied to college with nearly perfect scores on her S.A.T.'s, she was accepted at Yale and Duke—but rejected at the University of North Carolina. The school was affiliated with the state high school system, and in his letter of recommendation, the high school principal did not recommend Jean. "Plus at the time Carolina accepted only one woman for every four men," she said. "Any man could get in, but women couldn't."

She graduated Duke in three years, discovering subjects

ranging from sociology to bisexuality. "I was in college when I met some people who explained bisexuality to me, who showed that this was viable, that some people do it," she said. "From there it was a fairly short step to, This looks interesting to me."

Jean said she had no inkling of her sexuality before she went off to college. "We were totally caught up in science," she said, referring to herself and her high school beau, who followed her to Duke and is now a cosmic ray physicist at the University of Chicago. "I was totally oblivious to sex. Our idea of a fun time was to stay up all night and try to explode the backyard."

She had planned on becoming a research physician but each summer as she worked on the National Science Foundation grants that she was routinely awarded, she found herself frustrated and bored with the lack of immediate results. She ended up throwing the test tubes at the walls. Making money is what she really wanted to do.

In college, she would drive into the North Carolina countryside, buy old flapper dresses at Salvation Army stores for twenty-five cents, and sell them to the debutantes at Duke for twenty-five dollars. "Part of my drive is being one of four kids with never enough money around. I said to myself when I was little, I'm never going to be this poor. I can remember at the age of ten hearing my parents fighting about money and saying two things to myself: Birth Control, and, I'm going to be independently wealthy."

After graduating from Duke, Jean landed a job selling chemicals used in medical experiments in seven states in the Southeast. The chemical company transferred Jean to San Francisco where she established her social life around the Bisexual Center and became a member of its board of directors. She later met Rebecca Thomas, a Berkeley biochemist, who shared Jean's fascination with computers, and together they wrote *The User Guide to the UNIX System*, one of the best-sellers in the literature of computer software.

UNIX is a computer operating system that was developed by Bell Labs in 1969. An operating system is a crucial part of a computer. Sometimes called "the software soul," it's the

collection of instructions that coordinate the activity of
the computer hardware: the processor, disc drive, and the
printer. UNIX is notable as an operating system because it
can be transferred from one brand of computer to another
and from one model to another more easily than most other
systems.

Software is not yet standardized. Whereas all LP records
play at 33⅓, software, to use the record analogy, plays at
every speed from 33⅓ to 1000, and can only be used on
computers designed to play at its peculiar speed. Yates believes that when software becomes standardized, UNIX and
several other operating systems she studies will become the
33⅓, 45, and 78 of the industry. That's only her opinion.
Other experts dispute it. But to listen to Jean sing the
praises of software standardization at computer conven-
tions, you'd think it was a foregone conclusion.

"Yates has developed quite a reputation as being the true
believer in UNIX," said the computer reporter for one of the
nation's leading business magazines, with more than a
touch of sarcasm in his voice. "The microcomputer industry is full of true believers. Operating systems always
become objects of religious veneration. Jean did, on one occasion that I was told about but did not witness, deliver a
twenty-minute, frothing-at-the-mouth lecture on the vir-
tues of UNIX. She made a fool of herself."

According to those who attended that particular convention, Jean never made any such speech. But more important than the facts is the reporter's impression of her as
biased. "It undermines her credibility as an analyst of the
industry," he said.

That assessment is probably somewhat harsh. At a recent
press conference, reporters were writing down Jean's projections like eighth graders whose math teacher was giving
them the answers to the final exam. But Jean admits she
went overboard on UNIX. "When it first came out, I said,
'This is a phenomenon that we're going to have to see as
standard software.' Part of it is just that I didn't know
enough. Part of it is that the market was too muddy. It
wasn't clear how it was going to fall out."

Jean doesn't repent for long though. "People positioned
me. It was either black or white. There was no in-between.

So at a time when UNIX was practically unknown, the fact that I said, 'Here's a big phenomenon,' instead of taking it in the context in which I said it, people said, 'This woman's a fanatic about UNIX.'"

Jean has expanded her research beyond UNIX, and has taken up with another product called XENIX, a jazzier, easier-to-use version of UNIX, MS DOS, and CP/M, which are other potential standards. Both XENIX and MS DOS are produced by the Microsoft company, and Jean helps to promote them at industry outings. Though she sincerely believes they're the best, it gives the appearance of a conflict of interest when someone paid to assess an entire industry works with a specific product or company.

She says she appears at Microsoft functions and those of competitors, because she can't currently afford her own publicity, and they offer her exposure to the media. But even if she could afford an hour in prime time, chances are Jean Yates would still go wild when a wonderful new product hit the marketplace.

"Her natural personality is to zero in on one specific idea and to promote it almost to the death," said one of Jean's former bosses at Gnostic Concepts, another market research firm. "She's the same way with people; you're either tremendous in her eyes or you're nothing."

An associate at one company where Jean worked before starting her own firm recalls the problems Jean had with one of her bosses. "He had tremendous problems with Jean because she was too quick for him. He could not keep up with her intellectually," the associate said. "She lost respect for him and ran all over him. And she did it in a way that didn't have a lot of finesse. She would actively talk about his incompetence to other people, not quite to his face, but it would certainly get back to him."

Jean's version of events is slightly different, but, as always, in technicolor. "I had the bodaciousness to suggest that since I was selling most of the research in our department, I should make a higher salary than this twit who was sitting in the corner office making $60,000 a year because he was male and in his fifties," Jean explained. "They basically felt, No, he's fifty and plays the corporate game, so you're supposed to look up to him. And I said, I'll take my hundred grand a month in sales, thank you. And I did.

"I've deliberately sought out places where the rules hadn't been established yet," she added. "As my friends say, I love to live on the edge of the sword. I don't want it safe. I'll get bored in about two hours."

Perhaps the most objective assessment of Jean's abilities comes from the Japanese. "The Japanese are very demanding people in market research and basically very difficult to work with," a former associate at Gnostic Concepts observed. "In general, we had trouble meeting some of their standards. They prefer older people and they're not particularly fond of women. But Jean really took that in stride. When she went to Japan, she broke all sorts of records for the company in terms of orders booked."

Jean had what the Japanese demanded—massive quantities of knowledge. "It was sort of strange," she recalls fondly. "These tiny little Japanese men marauding down the street, and me clumping along behind carrying a hundred pound briefcase. It was a trip. I was like the great tortoise at the 1896 Chicago Exhibition. They just stared at me, which was fine. They all bought from me like crazy. You can be a woman if you're from the West. I was someone who knew a lot about what they wanted to know."

Another indication of Jean's talents is the devotion of her employees, several of whom are women who left Gnostic Concepts to come work for her. In a recent week, Yates Ventures' production manager put in over one hundred hours. "She's the kind of person you can give 100 percent and she knows you're giving 100 percent," she said. "You don't get the kind of double-talk where people say, 'Thank you and would you please. . . .' She knows what you're putting out. She won't give you quotas and say, 'I expect this standard.' She hires people she knows can produce the standard.

"She's a real good example of what's happening generationally," the production manager added. "One of the big reasons I enjoy working here is because everyone is individualistic and maintains a separate but very integrated viewpoint. We feel very strongly about the same kinds of issues. We all share an optimistic view of the future."

Jean is no slouch herself. "My only fear is that I'll burn out," she said. "For years I didn't push myself as far as I

could go. I'd say, These people think I'm doing okay, but
boy, I'm only using 25 percent of my energy. I have pushed
myself to the limit with this company. It's sort of scary.
There are days when I've said, There's so much to be done,
and I don't have an ounce of energy left."

The fear among her employees is not that she'll burn out,
but that with her weight, she'll have a heart attack. Jean
plays as hard as she works. She rented a hot tub club for the
office Christmas party, and brought the evening to a cre-
scendo when she joined her employees in a boisterous water
ballet.

When Jean recently moved to her new home in Los Altos,
one of her first purchases was nothing practical like bath
towels or a sofa, but rather a projection TV with a six-
foot screen. She describes herself as a "home-electronics
junkie."

Despite the occasional extravagance, Jean isn't a big
spender. Her income is a combination of the modest salary
she pays herself and royalties from *The User Guide to the
UNIX System*. It comes to about $50,000 a year. "The thing
I like about this job is not the money," she said. "If you like
the money and you like the prestige and you like the trappings, you'll never make it. What you have to like is the process. You have to like the agony of building it.

"I'm not going to take a whole lot of money out of the company," she added. "The whole thing is to make the company
grow. My goal when I was twenty-two was to be making
$100,000 a year when I was thirty. I met that goal when I
was twenty-seven. My new goal for when I'm thirty is to be
worth a million on paper. I'm worth about that right now
and I'm not thirty yet."

To Jean, Yates Ventures is but an apprenticeship for the
"big-time," which she projects will come around 1986 or
1987 "when I start the one I want to make $400 million on.
It's a question of how hard you want to work, and how long
you want to keep battling, because it's a continual battle."

She says she's startled at the resentment she's met in the
computer industry because of her success. "People come
out of the walls that hate your guts," she said. "These people say, 'I log into UNIX. Why aren't I famous?' I'll tell you
why. It's because you work unbelievably hard, and then

when it gets tight, you don't fold. The reason there aren't that many self-made millionaires is because it's very, very hard. You have to go into it working harder and being smarter than 99 percent of the population."

Jean's courageous attitude towards competition is reflected in her thoughts about the coming of artificial intelligence. "If something better comes along is that so horrible?" she questioned a reporter who expressed fears of being ruled by robots. "It's like being an American. There's nothing better than being an American. There's nothing better than being human. Ridiculous. There are things beyond that, and I don't see why we should be scared of them. It's great. We'll find our niche.

"I've found there are two attitudes people have toward life. I find myself in one camp and at odds with the other. My personal attitude is you work hard and honestly, and you get out of life what you put into it. On the other hand, there seems to be an attitude that instead of putting your energy into hard work, you put it into obstructing others heading in the same direction. I very strongly feel that those people are going to lose out. I believe what you put in will come back to you."

"When I was working at Gnostic Concepts, having someone with Jean's enthusiasm and drive and desire and commitment in many ways helped keep me going," a former boss said. "It wasn't that it was competition. Maybe in some ways it was. If I hadn't left and we'd both been there a year later maybe we would have had some competition."

"There's this quote that keeps coming back to me periodically as I'm driving up the freeway," Jean said. "It's 'Do not go gentle into that good night.' I just don't want to do it. When I stop moving and shaking and learning and growing I'll die."

Doug Schoen

Doug Schoen must have visited fifty supermarkets searching for votes the day before the special election to fill the congressional seat left vacant by the death of Queens Congressman Benjamin Rosenthal. He stalked the aisles in his grey suit and camel's hair coat until he found a potential voter and then announced, as if weary of the information himself after the six-week campaign, "Hi, I'm Doug Schoen. I need your help tomorrow."

The shoppers, most of them either old ladies or young mothers pushing baby carriages in this middle-class Jew- ish district, smiled politely at the candidate and then tried to maneuver around him to get at the pyramids of sale- priced toilet paper and laundry detergent. Most of them already knew all they needed to know about Doug Schoen, the twenty-nine-year-old "boy genius" who graduated from Harvard College and Harvard Law School, got an Oxford PhD at twenty-two, wrote a well-received biography of Senator Daniel Patrick Moynihan, and had advised Mayor Ed Koch, Israeli Prime Minister Menachem Begin, and twenty-two members of Congress while the president of his own polling firm. Doug had spent $280,000 of his own money on TV and radio advertising as well as on a 300-phone information bank to make sure they did know who he was.

"I saw you on TV," said one impressed grandmother, as she put down a cantaloupe and took Doug's hand in its place.

"I'm a good boy," said Doug, easing into the grandson role.

"I saw him on TV," the lady repeated. "I know all about him."

Doug disengaged his hand from her grip and headed out the door, making sure he hadn't missed anyone else. "Let's go," he shouted to his aide Dave O'Brien, who was handing out campaign literature on the sidewalk. Together they had clocked three thousand miles on the car's odometer in the last month alone, chauffeuring Doug from one supermarket to the next.

From the outset Schoen's election was a long shot. He didn't get the Democratic party nomination, and Governor Mario Cuomo dashed his hopes for the Liberal party line. Mayor Koch, whose career Doug had championed in the past, wished him the best of luck, but told him he was going to support the Democratic nominee.

"I'm an intelligent political analyst, a reasonably good judge of situations, a hard worker, and dedicated," said Doug, after the election. "Having said that how do you explain going off to run for Congress? A simple reason. I wanted to do it for about ten years. There was an opportunity. As a professional pollster I knew it was a long shot. Personally, I knew I had to live with myself after election day and I said, Look, you've got to try it. So I gave it my best shot and worked as hard as I could."

In addition to his political liabilities, Doug had some personal ones. He is not your typical telegenic candidate: His hair is thinning, his complexion pale, and he wears round, tortoise-shell glasses. He's also an uninspired campaigner. When he greets voters he looks bored. It seems as if he'd rather be hobnobbing with powerful friends at the Harmonie Club or playing squash at the Harvard Club. Not yet thirty, he gives the impression of someone more comfortable in smoke-filled rooms than standing in front of a crowd.

"Doug is not a natural anything," explained David Garth, the political media consultant, who has hired Doug and partner Mark Penn to poll for his clients. "He is not a naturally effusive guy. He's not a slap-on-the-back guy. He is much more cautious by instinct than he is open. He reminds me of Bill Bradley as a basketball player. Bradley didn't have a natural move in his body, but he's the kind of guy who would practice that jump shot from the left hand side seven hundred times. It's the same kind of discipline Doug has. He's not a natural politician as you saw. But he has the drive to force himself, the desire to achieve. That's the kind of drive decathalon champions are made of."

On election day, Doug had a feeling he was going to lose but even the political pollster in him hadn't guessed how badly. When all the votes were counted Doug received 5,983 compared to over 18,000 for the winner, State Senator Gary Ackerman. Each vote he had won had cost him about $50.

Doug didn't even stay up to watch the results on the eleven o'clock news. "I slept pretty well," he recalls without emotion. "I woke up at eight the next morning, took a shower, and was in the office by ten."

"I'm sure on some level the election defeat is more damaging than I'm letting on," he added, when pressed. "But I don't have any great sense on a day-to-day basis that it is."

The only change in Doug in the weeks after the election, noted Mark Penn, was that he arrived at work slightly later than usual and that he played squash more often than ever—as frequently as six times a week.

Doug attributes his defeat not to any lack of charisma but to "a structural situation that did not work to my advantage. Because of New York's election law, there was no Democratic primary. I was forced to run as an Independent against a Democratic candidate in an overwhelmingly Democratic district. It was not a rejection of me. It's not that I'm arrogant or tremendously egotistical. It's just if I do my best I'll generally succeed."

"Had there been a primary I think he would have won or come real close," David Garth said.

Garth was surprised at how well Doug took defeat. "I was amazed at his maturity," Garth said. "He made his race, did it in public, got killed, and recovered from it."

If there's any quality that separates Doug from the masses of other people his own age, it's that professional maturity—a willingness to work incredibly hard and to endure boredom and fatigue to achieve one's goals. "One of the striking things about him is that there was this maturity of organization at an astonishingly early age," said Bill Johnson, Doug's thesis advisor at Oxford. "He was like a well-organized executive of forty-five when he was twenty-two."

Doug completed his PhD thesis, a biography of the British racist Enoch Powell, in less than two years. It takes the average Rhodes scholar four to six years to complete the PhD requirements. His thesis was published as a book by Macmillan in 1977, and was praised for its contribution to race relations, on the front page of the *Times Literary Supplement*. Johnson attributes Doug's achievements more to perspiration than to inspiration. "As an intellect, he's not particularly stunning," Johnson said. "I teach an awful lot of Rhodes scholars. If I rank him against those guys, Doug is not in the top category. But once Doug has decided an area is something he's really interested in, people who are more intelligent than him quickly find Doug pulling ahead of them."

"He is not someone who writes well in any automatic way," Johnson added. "He needs someone to help him edit his stuff. But he plows through the raw material at such a rate that if he can get somebody to play that role. . . . I suppose a lot of the things I'm describing are rather like things that are said about the Japanese."

Doug's high school record at the Horace Mann School, one of the most competitive private schools in the country, was undistinguished. "I sort of see myself around the middle of the pack," said Doug of his intelligence. "I think I'm a person of above-average but not exceptional talent. I try and do a couple of things well." It probably helped his chances of getting into Harvard that his father, a high-powered New York lawyer, was an alumnus.

Doug offers no insight into his family and little more about himself. He is painfully private. If you ask him about experiences, he'll give you names and dates. You learn as much about him from speaking with him as you would by reading his resume.

At Harvard he came into his own. He became the muck-raking executive editor of the *Harvard Crimson,* a member of the board of directors of the Institute of Politics, and he graduated magna cum laude. "I realized I was able to take my interest in public affairs and really project myself," he said. "The strength of a Harvard education is not so much that it's a better school. It's not. But you have the capacity to meet people who can really draw you out."

Doug always had the rare ability to attract mentors. At Harvard it was political scientist Bill Schneider; at Oxford it was Johnson; professionally it's been David Garth; and personally Doug points to Congressman Steve Solarz. "I warmed to him because I'm so used to post-graduates who are sort of fopping around the place not quite getting down to things," Bill Johnson explained. "Doug is just so much the opposite. He made it clear early on that he was accepting you as an important person in his life and that your word was going to be terribly influential with him. You can't but help feel committed to a guy who is putting that much on the line for you."

Doug always had a knack of positioning himself where he could control information and power. "I got a sense of who the players were," he said of working at the *Crimson.* "When you're an undergraduate, you have a sense there's a large bureaucracy. You never meet anyone. And here I was calling the president. At least back then that was a pretty heady thing to do."

"Doug was always interested in controversy," said Mark Penn, who met Doug when they both worked on the *Crimson.* The politics of Afro-American studies was the primary target of Doug's pen, and he had professors at each other's throats.

"Racial issues were very prominent in the early seventies," Bill Schneider explained. "There was a lot of tensions and accusations, and Doug kind of dived into the thick of things. I'm not going to say he was enormously popular, because he used to embroil himself. There some some who thought he fueled the flames of controversy."

Doug even attacked the quality of the cuisine in the surrounding Cambridge area. "His most remembered piece was a review of a pizza parlor that had the owner shouting outside the *Crimson* offices," Mark Penn recalls, adding, "He's not interested in controversy today. He's much more conciliatory."

More important to Doug than questions of principle seemed to be the sport of influence-peddling. He was always the consummate politician. If the controversialist, the rabble-rouser, still exists in Doug, it's on sabbatical. But the politician remains and is more polished than ever.

Today, Doug plays everything close to the vest. Every response is measured. In the interval between a question and Doug's answer, you get the sense he's crafting his reply so it can't damage his career a dozen years down the road. When a reporter asks a question Doug considers perceptive, he starts to say it was a "good" question but then calls it "reasonable." "Reasonable" is a word Doug uses a lot. "I was reasonably open, reasonably straight," he said of his performance during the campaign. "I'm a reasonably good judge of situations," he remarked of his talents as a political scientist.

He's better than that. "His senior thesis was, in my opinion, brilliant," Bill Schneider said. "He graduated magna cum laude but I thought it was one of the best theses I ever supervised in my eight years at Harvard. Some of the readers, I thought, didn't quite grasp the brilliance of it."

At Oxford, Doug felt like an outsider and did nothing but work. When he wasn't researching his PhD thesis, he was commuting to London and working for the Labor Party's polling firm. "I think I was a bit of his defender in some senses," Bill Johnson said. "Some of the other people around, some of his peers thought of him as a bit of a monomaniac, a bit of a plastic man in the sense that he wasn't savoring things culturally or in depth or staying up all night to talk things over. He was just getting on.

"He was rather contemptuous of other postgraduates he was working alongside," Johnson added. "He would keep coming to me and say, 'Christ, these guys don't know what hard work is.'"

After Oxford, Doug enrolled at Harvard Law School because, he says, it was expected of him and because he didn't know what else to do. His reasons for attending Harvard Law sound uncharacteristically undirected and unpremeditated. But then, he didn't become a lawyer and set up a lucrative practice as he probably could have based on his own credentials and his father's connections. He did his work—"It wasn't much work, it took a couple of hours a week once you figured out how to get through it"—and searched for the next challenge. The challenge was the Moynihan biography that was published by Harper & Row in 1979. The *New York Times* called the book "a workmanlike biography" and added "the tone is favorable without being sycophantic; the style of the man if not conveyed as vividly as might be is suggested; no secrets are bared, few depths probed, but all bases are touched. . . ." It was a reasonable review.

Edward I. Koch, a congressman with no money and 6 percent name recognition, ran for mayor of New York in 1977 and hired David Garth to run his campaign. Ironically, it was only because Koch couldn't afford a name pollster like Peter Hart or Pat Cadell that Garth decided to give Penn and Schoen their big break. Doug had come to Garth's attention when he worked on Hugh Carey's 1974 gubernatorial campaign analyzing voting trends.

Since high school, Doug had worked on a succession of campaigns, and after his junior year in college, he had registered black voters in Mississippi on behalf of black gubernatorial candidate Charles Evers. "Doug was a political groupie who found a way to make a life and a business out of what fascinated him," Garth observed. "He's like a nymphomaniac in a whorehouse. If he wasn't getting paid for it, he'd do it for nothing."

Garth didn't pay much, and he made outrageous demands. "Because they hadn't worked for any other polling firm, they didn't have the built-in kinds of negatives," he explained. "If I told them I didn't want to wait two weeks for the returns, I wanted them in five days, they'd say, 'Okay, we'll get them in five days.'"

And sooner if necessary. Penn and Schoen employed a technique called *tracking;* they canvassed voters as frequently as every other day, allowing Garth to pick up the most subtle shifts in voter attitudes towards the candidates. The projections of "the kids," as Garth refers to his polling prodigies, were virtually without error, as they detected the rise of an obscure politican to become mayor of the largest city in the country. When Ed Koch was elected Mayor, Penn and Schoen's reputations were made as well.

Speed and accuracy became their trademark. On a weekend in 1980, Garth was called to Teddy Kennedy's home in Virginia to put the presidential candidate back together again after Roger Mudd had picked him apart during a "60 Minutes" interview. Teddy was to appear on "Meet the Press" the next day.

"When we finished the briefing, Steve Smith [Kennedy's campaign manager] said to me, 'We'll have to talk tomorrow after the show to see how he did.' I said, 'We don't want to know what we think; let's poll the country,'" Garth remembers.

At six o'clock on Saturday evening, he called Mark and Doug and arranged to have them interview 750 people before and after the show. "By twelve o'clock Sunday night, Steve Smith had in his hand a complete printout," Garth recalled with pride. "It really worked. He went up something like 24 to 27 points on Chappaquiddick."

In 1978 he sent them to Venezuela, a nation one political analyst had pronounced unpollable, and they called the election on the nose. In Israel two years ago Penn and Schoen polled for thirty-seven days, and the day before the election gave Prime Minister Begin a printout of the predicted results. They said it was going to be forty-seven seats each for the two major parties in the Knesset when the civilian vote was counted. They also predicted the Likud (Begin's party) would receive an additional 15,000 votes and an additional seat in the Knesset when the army vote was counted and would win the election.

David Garth recalled, "I let Doug and Mark hold a press conference with the Israeli press and the press said, 'Bullshit, don't tell us there's going to be over ninety seats to the two major parties. It never happened before.' When Prime Minister Begin landed in New York about six months after the campaign, the first thing he said to Koch was, 'I don't understand how those guys did it. They had it exactly.'"

"My personal goal as a Congressman will be as a spokesman for Israel both here and around the country," Doug told the members of the Queens Jewish Community Council during the campaign. Israel is one issue on which Doug displays uncharacteristic passion. He traces the roots of his activism to Oxford.

"When I was in England, I saw a great deal of hostility towards the State of Israel and anti-Semitism, and I'm someone who is deeply concerned that the State of Israel survive," he explained. "At St. Antony's [Doug's Oxford college] there were a large number of Arab students. One day a guy came up to me and said, 'You're a Zionist, aren't you?' At that point I really wasn't. I said, 'No, why do you say that?' And he said, 'Because you're a New York Jew.'

"I sort of thought to myself, 'If they're categorizing me as a Zionist because I'm a New York Jew, maybe I ought to be.' And that was at the same time Moynihan was talking at the U.N. about the Zionism resolution, which equated Zionism with racism, and that got me very upset."

When he returned to New York after Oxford, Doug joined the board of the Anti-Defamation League and did a study on anti-Semitic vandalism for the Simon Wiesenthal Center at Yeshiva University.

The traits commonly associated with the German Jews who immigrated to America a century ago—the pride, the drive—seem to have passed undiluted to Doug from his ancestors. In some ways, he's an old-fashioned fellow.

"About a year after the Evers campaign, Doug came through New Orleans, and I brought him out to my parents' house to have dinner," remembers Jason Berry, an Evers campaign co-worker. "At the time we had a dog named Calhoun, and I remember Doug asked my mother where Calhoun 'defecated.' She remembers that quite vividly because no one had ever used the word 'defecate' in connection with Calhoun.

"He's kind of old-fashioned in the way he conducts himself and relates to other people," Steve Solarz said. "He always pays attention to the niceties. I've never seen him
drunk. He's not a 'hail fellow well met' type."

Doug doesn't reveal a thing about his family, but his drive
seems to have its origins there. According to friends, Doug's
father is the kind of guy who would come home from the
office at 8:00 P.M., bring his attaché case to the dinner
table, and work while he ate. "His father was always ho-
hum about what we did," Mark Penn said. "He originally
thought we had no future in this work. Then he thought
the opposite. We had a future in this, but why was Doug
running for Congress."

Doug's parents were recently separated. "His mother is
terribly nice, a warm, friendly, sensitive person who, I
think, though she obviously loves Doug, is quite amused by
him," Bill Johnson said.

Needless to say Doug is tight-lipped about his personal
life. He dated one woman for several years, but is unattached at the moment. Politics is his constant mistress. "I
feel no compulsion to get married," he said. "If the prover-
bial right person came along, of course, I would not be re-
sistant. But, on the other hand, I don't feel my life is not
complete without being married. I have a much stronger
desire to be in Congress than to be married."

Doug has promised Mark Penn he'll devote his energies to
the business at least for the next couple of years. David
Garth believes that within the next five years Penn and
Schoen will become as important a force in the formulation
of American public opinion as Gallup, Harris, and Roper.
With Garth, Penn and Schoen are publishing the bimonthly
Garth Analysis, a national poll on a spectrum of issues.
They are also planning to get into direct mail. "I hope he
won't run again," said Garth sounding like a concerned uncle. "I've told him this. I think he can have a lot more influence and a lot more fun and certainly a hell of a lot more
money doing what he's doing now than as a freshman congressman."

Money and what it can buy seem to be low on the list of
Doug's priorities. Though he eats at the best restaurants
and belongs to the best clubs, his lifestyle is spartan. He

lives not in Manhattan but in Queens where he's established his political base. He commutes to work each morning on the subway. "My lifestyle is somewhat ascetic," he said. "I own a one-bedroom, modestly decorated co-op. I have no second home. I have not taken a vacation in over two years."

Doug refuses to discuss the finances of his company, but David Garth estimates that Penn and Schoen can clear $1 million a year. Asked if he'd ever tossed caution to the wind and bought anything truly extravagant, Doug smiled weakly and replied, "Yeah, a campaign."

Doug places himself to the left-of-center on the political spectrum and says he's "interested in the possibility of achieving some sort of social change." If Doug's an idealist, it's difficult to see it behind the hard-baked veneer of the political professional. Shrewdness predominates. David Garth believes Doug is an idealist but adds, "I think 99 percent of the people who know Doug would say he's not. I think the shrewd part of Doug is embarrassed by the idealistic part of Doug. Where he comes from—Harvard, where everyone has their own little scheme for power—it isn't smart to really be an idealist. There is something about it that is too unstructured."

Sometimes it seems that aristocracy, rather than democracy, is the political system best suited to Doug's personality. Those who know him best deny that he's arrogant, yet he's so ambitious the two become indistinguishable. "His energy knows no bounds, his commitment knows no bounds," Bill Schneider said. "Sometimes that can get him into trouble. It is possible to be too ambitious and too aggressive."

On the final day of his campaign for Congress, a local resident who supported the death penalty cornered Doug and asked him if he also supported it. He had publicly, but very quietly come out against it. "Are you for the death penalty?" the lady wanted to know. "Yes, but it's not something we're emphasizing," Doug mumbled in reply.

"I think he has an ambition to succeed which goes beyond commitment to good causes, which hasn't much to do with money, which goes beyond what I can trace in the fam-

ily background, which I can't fully explain and doubt
whether he can," Bill Johnson said. "It must be the secret to
him. It's tremendous motivation which powers him and
makes him work so hard."

Bill Schneider has a theory. "He's basically a pol," Schneider said. "He loves the game, he's committed to the game,
he wants to win the game."

Jeffrey
Hollender

While other little kids watched TV shows like "Sky King" and "My Friend Flicka" on Saturday mornings in the late 1950s, Jeffrey Hollender sat in his father's office and screened toy commercials. "We'd have the whole sales department and management there sitting in the back and looking at him," recalled Jeff's father Alfred Hollender, who was president of Grey Advertising, the seventh largest agency in the world. "He'd say, 'I don't understand what you're talking about,' and we'd scrap a commercial because obviously we'd missed the boat. Or he'd say, 'Gee, I like that one, but I don't like the toy.' We made many marketing changes based upon his reactions. They eventually turned out to be right, because our commercials scored very well with the kids."

At twenty-eight, Jeff hasn't lost any of that instinct for what his peer group wants. In 1979, he founded Network for Learning, an innovative continuing-education program that offered New Yorkers courses that combined information and entertainment, as well as a casual setting to meet members of the opposite sex. By its second year, Network was grossing $1.5 million on an initial $60,000 investment thanks to 50,000 students a semester who sincerely wanted to know "How to Marry Money," "How to Lose Your Brooklyn Accent," and "How to Get Invited to the Right Parties."

"One of the major trends that makes this possible," said Jeff sitting in his wide-windowed office, "is people wanting to spend money on the quality of their lives rather than on the accumulation of material possessions. People don't want to reupholster their sofas in the 1980s. They want to buy a vacation at Club Med."

When Network was getting off the ground, Jeff found ideas for courses everywhere. If he was at a party and a friend complained about not being able to find an apartment, Jeff would offer a course on finding apartments. If he had a great meal at a fancy restaurant he'd ask the owner to teach a course on opening your own restaurant. "He can look at society and perceive what the needs of that society are," said Jeff's younger brother, Peter Hollender. "I guess it stems from a good understanding of himself."

In conversation Jeff is constantly objectifying, analyzing himself and his emotions and how he fits into the world. "He doesn't know how to relax," said Peter. "He can never completely dismiss the world. He can never lose touch with reality. He's too plugged in to what he's about—his goals, his dreams, his desires."

Jeff has experimented with virtually every kind of therapy, from primal scream to transactional analysis. But he is not morose or overly self-involved. He has that rare ability to separate himself from his success. "Business is acting," he observed. "If you were from the *Wall Street Journal*, I wouldn't discuss my personal conflicts or my personal ambition. I'd present you with a very solid business success story.

"I am a performer. If I wanted to make a deal with you, I'd get you to want to make a deal with me. I'd make you feel that I'm tremendously successful, because people always want to be involved with successful people.

"Today, before you came, I said to myself, 'Gee, I'm going to get interviewed now. Do I want to provide him with some hot material that would sound great in the book or do I want to be totally honest?' I said, 'Hell, I'm tired of spewing out this bullshit for people.' I hate giving interviews now because it's all presenting this image of success and money."

There's a lot of Jeff, the searching humanist as well as the savvy entrepreneur, in Network For Learning's catalogue. As *Time* magazine noted, "Network's phenomenal success is due, in large measure. to Hollender's shrewd ability to live off the fad of the land."

"Lady Di does it, so did Snow White, Cleopatra, even Prince Charming," starts the course description for "How to Flirt," one of the Network's typically upbeat and alluring offerings. "Scarlett O'Hara wasn't batting those baby blues for nothing. She was practicing an art that's as old as time, as fun as ice cream, and as tactical as tennis. From the butterfly touch to the teasingly titillating smile, men and women will learn how to capture the attention of that stranger across the room, beckon that someone special out for a date, cash a check with a butcher . . ."

Jeff and his staff often invented courses at brainstorming sessions that lasted late into the night. The scene was highly reminiscent of staff-writer bull sessions for "Saturday Night Live." During those red-eyed hours, Jeff came up with some of his most sensible courses—"How to get a Credit Card"—and some of his silliest—"On Sunday the Rabbi Ate Pork"—an irreverent look at Jewish humor.

For the first couple of years that Network was in operation, Jeff lived on very little sleep. "I'd work on Friday night and say, 'I'm going to take it easy tomorrow.' And then on Saturday morning I'd get a call that the bus didn't show up to take the people hot air ballooning, and they're standing on the corner fuming, and it's five degrees out, and what should we do?

"And I'd have to get dressed and walk over there even though I'd only slept two hours, and say, 'I'm sorry, here's money to take a cab home.' I remember one time taking everyone out to breakfast. Some guy had taken the train from Philadelphia. Someone else had come from Chicago. These people were really angry. You have to extend yourself in a very personal way, because you're dealing with these people's lives and their free time. And that's a very delicate thing and you assume a huge responsibility."

Despite the occasional setback, Network proved so successful that by 1982 the field was flooded with imitators, and Jeff had to scramble for his own students. "It's been rough," Peter Hollender said. "He's had a seemingly dreamy future collapse. When he started this thing he had no competition. Now there are programs all over the place that have taken off on his ideas."

Jeff was forced to give up his suite of offices in midtown and run his business out of his apartment. But he seems to be on the road to recovery. He's made a couple of deals whose impact, both financially and societally, may dwarf Network's classroom business eventually. He signed a deal with Walden Books to distribute audio tapes based on Network courses in seven hundred of their stores as well as those of other national retailers, including Sears and Woolworth. He's also entered into a co-venture with Warner-Amex to bring Network to cable TV.

Jeff attributes his rebounding ability less to shrewd business deals than to a fundamental view of the world. "People's lives are self-fulfilling prophecies," he said. "If you believe you're going to be a failure, goddamn it, you're going to be a failure. If you believe you're going to be a success you have a much better chance of becoming successful."

As a child, Jeff said, his parents traveled frequently and he was raised by nurses. He spent a lot of time alone, and he believed loneliness to be the only authentic state of existence. Friendship, happiness, love were all myths.

But Jeff said that he had gotten help from a man who had been his fifth-grade teacher. Jeff met him again in recent years, and this man became his "spiritual counselor." "He helped me move from a world that was cold, hostile, and lonely to a world that was warm and friendly— not because the world is hostile and lonely or warm and friendly. He helped me realize the world was both, and that I had a choice. I can create a hostile world or I can create a friendly world. He gave me the power to realize I can create what I want to create."

Taking off in unexpected directions is something Jeff has been doing since adolescence. He attended Riverdale Country School in the Bronx, but dropped out when he was fifteen to go surfing in Florida, and again when he was sixteen to move to California to live with an older woman. His parents' marriage was on the rocks, and life at home was miserable.

The family was wealthy. They lived in a fourteen-room apartment on Park Avenue, but Jeff's father refused to give him a cent to run away. That didn't deter the boy. He headed west in a small station wagon he'd bought with the earnings from a summer window-washing enterprise, and picked up a hitchhiker in Oklahoma who helped pay for gas. He arrived on the West Coast penniless. After only three days, Jeff and his woman friend fell out of love, and he had to live in his car for several months.

Stories like these typically end with the spoiled child rushing home to Mommy and Daddy. Jeff didn't. He made money gardening and washing windows and even enrolled himself at Santa Barbara High School where he received his first "A" ever. It was for a course entitled, "How to Balance Your Checkbook."

Eventually Jeff returned home, graduated from high school, and entered Hampshire College, an experimental school in Massachusetts. It wasn't experimental enough for Jeff. "I was in college a year and a half, and I spent four months writing a paper that one person was going to read," he recalled. "So I said, Why should I spend four months devoting all my energy to something that's going to be read and graded by one person? It just didn't make sense to me personally, because that's not the way I aspired to lead my life. I felt like I had something to say. First of all I didn't want to say it for the grade. Secondly, I didn't want to say it to just one person."

Authority, particularly submission to it, is something that's never sat well with Jeff. "They always told me in school I had a problem with authority," Jeff said. "I have a problem with authority in that it tells people what to do without them understanding it. That's destructive.

"My father was a very outspoken, authoritarian type of person—the kind who said, When I tell you to do something, do it! And I revolted against that early on. I discovered that the solution was to say back to him, 'Forget it.'"

Network for Learning began as a "skills exchange" in Toronto. Jeff happened upon the idea of a skills exchange in Ivan Illich's *Deschooling Society* and became fascinated with it. He saw it as the antidote to his own disastrous experience with education. Jeff's other reason for starting the exchange was less cosmic. He had followed a girlfriend to Toronto and needed something to do.

In that respect Jeff seems different from most other very successful young people who are willing to suspend their personal lives in pursuit of visions of grandeur. Personal milestones are as precious to Jeff as professional ones. His most important relationship is not to the public, but to a few close friends, his brother, his girl friend, and perhaps most importantly, to his father.

At first the Canadian government balked at the idea of allowing a foreigner into the country to start a skills exchange. They assumed the venture would fail. They were wrong. In its first year, the exchange grossed $250,000 on a $3,000 investment. It also became an instant focal point, a kind of clubhouse, for community-spirited young people in Toronto.

The government started to sing a different tune. Any business that successful ought to be run by a Canadian, they said, and they tried to force Jeff to abandon the business. One member of Parliament thought the government's treatment of the American so unfair, he denounced their action on the floor of Parliament. Jeff became a cause célèbre. The Toronto *Star* ran a front-page and full-page stories about him. But eventually the government prevailed and forced Jeff to sell the business. It is still in operation.

Jeff believed if the concept played in Canada it would also play in New York. His father was skeptical but agreed to lend him part of the $60,000 Jeff estimated it would take to launch the program in the Big Apple. Jeff had to attract outside investors, so he wrote an eighty-page prospectus that was executed so professionally that lawyers who examined the document were convinced it was written by other lawyers.

Jeff's performance should have surprised no one, particularly his father. Brother Peter can't forget the way Jeff used to slave over his homework as a child. "He would take two hours to do the same assignment it would take me half-an-hour to do," Peter remembered. "He might have been able to do it in half-an-hour, but he had a desire to be perfect. He was so scared of not being good."

But Jeff's father wasn't the easiest guy in the world to please, not even after his son's stunning success. "Here I was, I had a school with forty thousand students and two hundred teachers working for me, and he would call me up and say, 'Some day you're going to be interviewed and they're going to ask you where you went to college, and you're going to be embarrassed to say you didn't graduate.' And he hammered away at me until I said, 'Dad, I'll write my own degree, Okay.'"

Eventually the company's success brought the two men closer. Jeff calls his father several times a week asking for advice, and if Alfred Hollender feared his son's success might be fleeting, the older man's contemporaries keep reminding him that the kid had a lot more on the ball than one good idea. Recently a friend of Jeff's father who is a partner at the investment banking firm Brown Brothers called to tell Al about a meeting he had arranged between Jeff and a couple of other partners at the investment house.

"They're pretty tough guys," said Hollender senior, his voice ringing with pride, "and when Jeff left the room to get something, one of them turned to the other two and said, 'This youngster's a genius.'

"He knew as much about business as the backside of an elephant when he started," Hollender added. "But he sure learned a hell of a lot in the last five years. Today he knows twice as much about business as I did at his age, and then some. And I thought at that time I was a reasonably good businessman."

In October, Jeff's father suffered a massive heart attack. Jeff devoted himself to his father's recovery, canceling appointments, forfeiting business opportunities, and neglecting his friends. "It makes me cry to see how attentive he's been," said Alfred Hollender. "Whatever you want to talk to me about business is nothing compared to the way he's conducted himself while I've been ill. He couldn't have done more if he were part of me."

Jeff has literally been losing sleep wondering how he's going to convince the world's experts to teach his courses on cassette. He's not interested in some hack writer teaching a course that might hypothetically be called, "How to Sell a Novel to Television." He wants Herman Wouk. He won't settle for some accountant to explain, "How to Balance Your Checkbook," unless he's been turned down by David Rockefeller twice.

Jeff paced the pavement in front of his girlfriend's apartment house at three and four in the morning last autumn, scheming about how he was going to persuade Rabbi Harold Kushner, the author of the bestselling book *When Bad Things Happen to Good People*, to make a tape based on the book. "But he's turned down all kinds of people," Jeff explained. "I've got to be honest with him. I'll tell him, 'You can look at this tape as reaching a lot of people who can't read or won't read, who when they're going through some kind of trauma can't focus on your book. So maybe this tape is another way of helping people.'" The rabbi succumbed to Jeff's reasoning and recently signed a contract with him.

It's also a way of making Jeff and the rabbi a lot of money. According to Jeff, his company is today worth "several million dollars" and he or members of his family own 40 percent. It has provided him with a life-style that allows him to own three cars and a co-op apartment. He eats in the finest restaurants in New York City, and takes off for St. Barts, a tiny paradise in the Caribbean, whenever he gets the urge.

But Jeff sees a certain shallowness to his success. The scales fell from his eyes when he appeared on the Phil Donahue show. He was accompanied by Joan Steichen, the creator of his course, "How to Marry Money." "Phil Donahue didn't take a stand, but what he did was try to agitate the hell out of the audience," recalls Jeff, who is disturbed by the experience a year later. "He tried to generate their anger and their frustration and their feeling of, 'This is wrong; you shouldn't marry for money.'

"And I found myself taking all my charm and all my intelligence and devoting it to reinforcing and rationalizing this concept of how to marry money. And I walked out of the show and I said, What the hell am I doing? Why am I flying to Chicago to support this thing? Maybe I'm getting a little bit off the track. It was a bizarre experience. I knew it was a major turning point."

Actually, it was a minor turning point. "I got sucked back into the excitement of what I was doing and didn't react to that experience. You know I'm young and it's very easy to get dazzled by the world," he said apologetically. "It's easy to get dazzled by meetings with Warner-Amex and being interviewed by the *Times* and all that stuff. It's truly exciting to pick up a newspaper, to see your picture in it, and to read what you said. It's very easy to lose touch with all kinds of things, with friends as well as with your own ethics and morals. This whole thing with money, it's like quicksand."

Jeff's conscience is like the Pioneer space probe. Long after it might have died, it keeps sending back messages. "I saw a bum crawling on his hands and knees while on my way to work this morning, and I thought, what are they going to say in the future about a culture like ours that lets people die in the street while spending millions on defense?

"It is absolutely my fault and I contribute to it as much as anybody," he said. "That's why I live with a lot of confusion. I have fallen into that category of being part of the greatest evil at times."

Jeff's misgivings towards his own success are illustrated by his attitude toward publicity. "At first if he saw stories about himself in the newspapers he'd get very excited," Alfred Hollender recalled. "In the next phase he'd just send me a photostat. And in the third phase I'd never know about it unless I'd see it somewhere myself."

"I knew Sheila a long time before I showed her a picture of myself in *People* magazine," said Jeff refering to his girl friend. "In business you're always presenting an image. But in a personal sphere if you present that image, what you get back is bullshit."

After 5:00 P.M. Jeff is full of courage and compassion. He once carried a homeless man to a hospital, and recently he agreed to testify against an off-duty cop whom he saw shoot a man who was lying in the street, though other witnesses walked away. "If I can't do something in my business, I'll always do something outside my business to participate in the human race," he said.

Jeff's goal is to do something virtuous for a living, to not feel as if he has to atone for his success after leaving his office. What has given him greater satisfaction than anything else he's accomplished in the last few years is a Network ethics course that he developed and taught himself, entitled, "Right and Wrong: Bending the Rules in Everyday Life." Students who enrolled brought their own questions and conflicts: A woman wanted to know if she should feel guilty because she enjoyed making love to men other than her husband. A man wondered if he should accept a raise from a company he was about to quit.

"Where do people turn to ask a question like that," Jeff wonders. "There is no authority any more. I've tried to understand for myself if we're at a unique point in the absence of authority.

"I've shown myself I have the ability to organize things, to make things happen on a relatively large scale," he added, looking at his career as if it were a question before his ethics class. "Now the issue for me is what direction I apply that to. And the direction is not fundamentally going to be making money. How I get from the development of these skills to what I believe in, I'm really not sure. That's something I'm struggling with right now."

Joan Jett

Photo by Ricky Byrd

Kenny Laguna, *the manager of Joan Jett and the Black-*
hearts, is the only one who seems to know or care that it's
costing $150 an hour to rent the Kingdom Sound recording
studio on Jericho Turnpike in Long Island, New York. Members of the band are playing video games in the studio's living room while Joan sits by herself in the studio practicing
a riff on her electric guitar.

"She may not be worth anything in a year but right now
her time's at a premium," says Kenny as he frantically leads
a reporter who is an hour late to meet Joan. Joan's song, "I
Love Rock-n-Roll" was the number-one song in the country
for seven weeks in 1982 and her album *Bad Reputation*
went double platinum—it sold over two million copies.

Joan seems in no rush to start the interview. She continues to practice, her fingers sliding up and down the strings of the guitar making music that resonates at 150 decibels from a wall of speakers behind her. When she's finally satisfied with the sound she puts the instrument down, takes a swig from a can of Diet Pepsi, and leads the way to the mixing room overlooking the studio.

She looks like a Hollywood version of a street kid. She wears cowboy boots, jeans with a set of keys hanging off them, a red denim version of a motorcycle jacket with zippers everywhere, a thick black leather bracelet with silver studs, and lots of make-up, especially eye liner. But her features are beautiful—a small nose, soft brown eyes, and full, well-formed lips, all of it framed by jet black hair cut into a shag. Joan said the name *Jett* is her mother's maiden name. She didn't make it up.

"I used to go to concerts starting around age eleven in Rockville, Maryland, and I started playing guitar at twelve," she said. Her voice has a hoarse defiance to it, like a tomboy who learned to defend herself in playgrounds. "I thought then that I'd like to be on stage, to play to an audience. It wasn't so much the thing of fortune and the limousines and all that stuff. It was being on the stage that was the main thing. Everything else would be like a fringe benefit."

"Being on the radio's a bigger rush than being a rock star," interrupts Kenny who is never very far away from Joan. "It's a certain thing of being part of the history, being on the radio, being a part of the important subculture."

A word about Kenny. At thirty-four, he has lived on the fringes of rock 'n' roll his whole adult life. In the mid-sixties he was a journeyman musician playing with groups like Tommy James and the Shondells, Jay and the Americans, and Ohio Express. More recently, he produced road shows for the play *Beatlemania* and records for New Wave artists such as Greg Kihn and Steve Gibbons. Rock 'n' roll is art, sports, politics, and religion all rolled into one for Kenny, and he's bitter because he says it's been stolen from the true believers and paganized by corporate clones "in their Gucci chains."

To Kenny, Joan is the great young hope of rock 'n' roll, the keeper of the flame, a performer of passion whose power to uplift her audience continues a tradition that started with Elvis. To Kenny, Joan is a national treasure, a culture hero. He spends most of his time trying to convince everyone else he's right.

"For Kenny rock 'n' roll is religion, and Joan is the personification of rock 'n' roll," explained rock publicist Howard Bloom, who advised Kenny on Joan's career for several years. "She's the spirit of defiance against anyone who ever tried to crush you."

"Rock 'n' roll freed our generation. It was communication. It was the way kids were able to talk to each other," Kenny ranted. He speaks with a thick Brooklyn accent and looks like the target market for adult jeans. "It was the way we protested the war. How much of a protest would there have been without rock 'n' roll? It's a major thing. It is religion. And the problem is people are screwing with it. This phony disco that's out now is not rock 'n' roll. The menace, the anger, the alienation, the frustration of youth is in rock 'n' roll."

Joan nods silently while Kenny continues his tirade, like a younger sister deferring to her older brother. Offstage, Joan is out of her element. She seems in a state of suspended animation, not much interested in conversation or ideas. She is a creature not of the mind but of the body. Kenny does most of the talking. Still, Joan is street smart and self-confident and can hold her own with anyone. When she wants to say something, Kenny shuts up. That's part of the deal. Joan's the boss. You don't mess with the gods.

"From the time the Runaways broke up it was like, 'Forget Joan Jett,'" said Joan, referring to the band that helped establish her "bad reputation" back in 1975 and almost killed her career. "I had the least chance of probably anybody in the world of getting signed to a record contract. To wind up with a number one single, and records that went gold and platinum just blows my mind. It just leads me to believe a lot of kids must be pretty bored with the music they're hearing. If they want to hear some good old basic rock 'n' roll, then we're the band to see, because that's what we play, that's what we like to play, and that's what we'll continue to play."

After the Runaways disbanded, twenty-six record companies rejected Joan when she approached them about recording on their label. "It's a classic rock 'n' roll story," Kenny said. "The biggest joke is to come out of all this hopelessness and bullshit. Every expert in the world said we couldn't have a hit record. To come out of it and get a number one record with a song called 'I Love Rock-n-Roll'! If you wrote a book like that people would say, 'What, are you kidding? It's too phony.'"

Kenny spends a lot of time sanding and polishing the legend of Joan Jett. But he has a lot to work with. The Runaways, the band Joan helped create, consisted of five girls whose average age was fifteen. Dressed neck-to-toe in leather, they looked like every father's nightmare of what his daughter would turn out to be if she weren't home by eleven.

To the rock establishment they were nothing but jailbait. "Some place in every interview you knew there was going to be a sex question," Joan remembers. "It was so depressing because I sat there and I kept thinking, 'When are they going to ask me about the music?'"

Joan was the lightning rod who attracted much of the negative publicity aimed at the group. "I was always the big mouth in the Runaways," she said. "I have a bad temper. I pop off real fast. If somebody asks me a question that sounds a little bit loaded I want to know exactly what they're asking me before I answer."

Eventually the other members of the band ganged up on her. Maybe they thought by eliminating the source of controversy, they could salvage their own reputations. Or maybe they were just jealous that Joan stood out, that she had star potential. "It got weird and I got the vibe they were going to fire me from a band I was first in," Joan said. "Nobody's going to fire me from a band I was first in. I didn't even try to hang on an extra couple of weeks to see if they would change their minds. *I* made the decision to quit the band. I said, 'I quit.'"

"She was an artist who was having gold and platinum records when she was fifteen years old," explained a business associate. "And by the time she was seventeen, she was already a has-been. It's a strange experience to go through at that age. She saw friends who had been ever so chummy one year, the next year wouldn't return her calls."

But it wasn't as if Joan ever considered doing anything other than playing rock 'n' roll. "I knew no other way of life," she said. "I didn't want to go back home and work at McDonalds."

Joan grew up in a middle class family that moved from Maryland to Los Angeles when she was fourteen. Her father was an insurance agent and her mother worked as a doctor's secretary. They didn't second-guess her when she dropped out of school to join a band. It would have been equivalent to the Kent family trying to force Superman to trade commodities instead of fighting a never ending battle for truth and justice and the American way.

"I could throw a ball farther than anybody in my school when I was in grade school," Joan recalled. "I was very good in sports. I was always a leader. When I would hang out with kids, it would always be me who would decide what games to play—not by force but because everyone looked to me to find out what we wanted to do."

Whatever bonds Joan may have to her parents, to her younger brother who works in a lumber yard, and to her younger sister who attends an agricultural college in California, they don't seem important in terms of her career. "Everyone seems to carry around a cast of characters in their head to whom they're playing," Howard Bloom observed. "For Joan I don't see any cast of characters."

Never seriously having considered going home after the Runaways disbanded, Joan slapped together a band that was neither talented nor well-rehearsed and took them to Europe where they performed in some of the roughest clubs, for some of the most crazed punks on the planet. In Germany, motorcycle thugs would interrupt the show shouting, "Do you love the Fuhrer?" Joan would tell them to screw themselves and keep playing—or start fighting. She left the choice up to them.

She tried to compensate for her inferior band by throwing every ounce of energy and passion behind her voice and her guitar. At night, dressed in the leather garb she'd worn on stage, she'd sleep on people's floors. The band sneaked into hotels and stole food from room service trays left out in the hall. For her dedication, she got pneumonia and was sent back to a hospital in America.

"Everyone asks, 'How do you get into a famous band?'" Joan says without cynicism. "You starve to death. You work your ass off and you crawl through the trenches and the mud, and you get stepped on and you take a lot of crap. And you take it. And you fight however your instincts tell you to fight back."

Soon after she was released from the hospital, Joan met Kenny. "My wife was the one who told me to go out and meet Joannie," Kenny recalled. "She said, 'She's significant.' My old lady knows. She's a very well educated person in rock 'n' roll.

"She didn't have a very refined look," Kenny remembered of his first encounter with Joan, who was twenty pounds heavier then. "She was definitely showing the effects of being a street kid. Her pants were all baggy, and she was poor, disgustingly poor, but she was beautiful to me. She was androgynous to me always. She had that thing where she sat in the middle like Jagger and Bowie.

"I knew she was going to have hit records because she did something to me. I told her that the second day we were together. I told my friend Richie [Richie Cordell who wrote and produced such hits as "Mony, Mony" and "Gimme, Gimme Good Lovin'"] I'm going to be partners with her and he said, 'You been taking Quaaludes?'"

"There were good vibes from the start. We locked in like a little combat unit," Joan recalled, and added, "I wasn't looking to make enemies. I was thinking, Maybe these are guys who can help me out."

She wasn't about to sell her soul though. Joan may have been living on borrowed luck when Kenny and Richie agreed to go to London and help her record the *Bad Reputation* album on the German Ariola label with ex-Sex Pistols Steve Jones and Paul Cook, but when Kenny told her to just sing and to leave the guitar playing to studio musicians, Joan refused flat-out. "I said, 'I play on the basic track or there's no record,'" she recalled. "I was getting the vibe like, 'she's a girl and she's not good enough.'"

As an import, *Bad Reputation* sold 22,000 copies within weeks of its release and went to the top of the charts at stations like Los Angeles's KNAC and Long Island's WLIR. *Creem* magazine called Joan, "quite frankly, a great rock 'n' roll singer," and the *Village Voice* described the album as "blunt, funny, and sexy."

The only people who weren't enthusiastic were the record company executives. Perhaps her image from Runaway days still got in the way, or her raspy voice which sounded nothing like the slick, pre-packaged sound that was popular in 1980, or her lyrics which sounded like she was giving them all the finger. "I don't give a damn about my reputation," she sang on *Bad Reputation.* "You're living in the past / It's a new generation / And a girl can do what she wants to do / and that's what I'm gonna do."

"You should see all the letters we got back from all those bigwigs about Joannie not having the class to be on their record label," Kenny said.

Kenny and Joan decided to cut a record on their own. Joan hocked everything she owned, and Kenny used the nest egg he'd set aside for his infant daughter's education. The pressure to succeed was so great Kenny landed in the hospital with migraine headaches. The doctors told him, "You better give up whatever you're doing because it's killing you."

But at the same time they were developing a following. Joan hit the road in New York and New England with a band she'd hired. "She got out there and the audiences began to respond instantly," a business associate recalls. "She'd play a club, and the club owner would call up the next day and say he'd never seen the audience respond so warmly. And he'd offer her more money whenever she wanted to come back. Within two months she moved from being an act nobody was particularly interested in to being somebody who could headline any club she wanted to in the Northeast."

Disc jockeys also sensed the rapport between Joan and their audiences. *Bad Reputation* became the ninth most played album on FM radio, competing for air time at the height of the Christmas season against the Goliaths of rock 'n' roll—The Eagles, Bruce Springsteen, and Steely Dan.

It was at a concert at New York's thirty-five hundred seat Palladium that Joan Jett and the Blackhearts made it clear to the rock 'n' roll establishment, many of whom were there, that she was a force to be reckoned with. Joan was just the opening act for a group called XTC, but as soon as she appeared on stage, the audience jumped to their feet cheering and stood throughout her entire set. And when she stopped many people in the audience didn't even stay to hear the headliner.

"She ate them up," Kenny said. "She blew them away. Suddenly everyone was patting me on the back."

"She can't move anywhere without security," said Kenny with concern but also with elation. *People* magazine selected Joan one of the twenty-five most intriguing people of 1982.

"I went to Roosevelt Mall the other day and it was like walking into the audience," Joan said. "I was looking for a book on slide guitar, and I walked into a music store. Literally, within seconds, seventy-five to a hundred kids were around us jabbing pens at me."

"We went food shopping," Kenny continues. "Before we got done there were thirty kids waiting outside. I don't know where these kids come from; they're like bugs." Kenny said that whenever Joan ventures into Manhattan, "she goes with heavy security, two killers."

Kenny and Joan live in separate homes within shouting distance in Long Beach, Long Island, a middle-class beach suburb. Whenever Joan wants to leave her house she calls Kenny who comes over to escort her out. "Right now we're living in fear for her. The hundred yards that separates us makes me nervous," Kenny explained. "In the house we're living at, there are people crawling up the stairwells.

"We're moving to some property where there's a fence around it," he adds, being intentionally vague about its location lest the interviewer be a stair-crawler himself. "There's a mania attached to rock 'n' roll."

Joan says the frenzy she inspires in her fans, some of whom dress and cut their hair to look like clones of her, doesn't frighten her. "It goes along with the spontaneity and the dangerousness of rock 'n' roll," she said. "When you're doing a show, you've got the kids on the edge of a riot because you're on the edge of a riot yourself."

"We've done class gigs though," adds Kenny who hopes Joan will eventually be loved by everyone, not just the young and the restless. "We played for the Communist Party heads in East Germany. We were really polite. We were great ambassadors. We created more good will than Reagan does."

Much as he brags about the East German tour today, he opposed it at the time. The money was just starting to roll in. Kenny had his heart set on buying a house, and he estimated a European tour would cost the band $100,000. How can you blame the guy? He'd put his kid's college education on the rock 'n' roll of the dice. He was owed.

"Joan said, 'I don't care,'" recalled Howard Bloom. "She said, 'Where's all the money? We're supposed to be big. Screw the house. I don't need a house.' And she doesn't need a house. She's always on the road."

"I didn't get into this for money," Joan explained. "Like I said, the dream was to be on stage, not necessarily the fortune. I've been poor before."

She may never be poor again. When *Bad Reputation* was re-released in 1981 by Boardwalk Records it sold over 2 million copies. "A million seller is $10 million gross," Kenny said. "So the record company gets their share, but Joan is in control of her own fate. She's a big owner of the company. She'll make a lot of money as will I."

She has few possessions though. Her only extravagance is the bathroom she's designing in the house with the fence around it. "It's worked around stuff I had to do," she said, feeling the need to make excuses for spending money. "There's steam for my throat and a whirlpool for my muscles, because I get extremely sore."

Joan has a weekly allowance of $175. It's a good sum of spending money but nothing compared to what your average rock star can make vanish in a night when he sets his mind to it. "I don't live beyond my means," Joan said.

"We live way below our means," Kenny quickly adds in case anyone got the impression this rock star had a cash flow problem. "The bills are paid. If we want to go stay at the Plaza we stay there. If we want to go to Hawaii for two weeks we do."

Joan said she doesn't feel confined having Kenny involved in every aspect of her life. "He's protecting me because I was completely unprotected while I was in the Runaways," she said. But she is in control of her own life. Once Kenny and she had a fight, and Joan knocked him out cold. On another occasion, he wanted her to perform at a fund-raising benefit for Teddy Kennedy when he ran for President in 1980, but she refused. Instinctively, she seems to know what's right for her.

In one of her videotapes, Joan flashes a taut, bikinied body from under a trenchcoat. When Howard Bloom saw the tape he panicked. He thought Joan was blowing her hard won "Bad Reputation" and was falling back into the stereotypical role of the victimized female. He was wrong. "I've talked to women, and they love it," Bloom said. "They say, 'Look at the way she's doing that. She's not doing it like a victim. She's daring you, man.' They thought it was a gesture of defiance. And that's what Joan's about—gestures of defiance."

For all her stage sexuality and the stories in tabloids that have linked her to men on four continents, Joan doesn't have a boyfriend. "It's hard to have a boyfriend on the road," she said. "The guy I was seeing is in the Bahamas or someplace."

Joan has been on the road for three years, almost without interruption, and has performed anywhere from 400 to 700 shows, depending on who you ask. "I'm too much of a gypsy; I can't stay in one place," she said. "I've been living out of my suitcase since I was fifteen. I'm used to it."

"She came off the road in December. She had just finished up in Australia and Hawaii, and I ran into her in an office on the other side of town," Howard Bloom said. "After three years and 618 dates around the world she'd finally spent two weeks in the same place. But she was slumped in a chair looking bored. I asked her how things were and she said, 'Man, I can't take it anymore. I can't take just sitting around. I've got to get back out on the road.'"

This perpetual motion makes some of her experiences seem like glimpses caught from a passing train. Several months ago Joan opened for The Who at a concert in Orlando, Florida. She was on her way from East Germany to Japan at the time, and she speaks about the experience as if it happened in a dream. "All I could do was picture a map of Florida and a dot that said Orlando," she said. "And then, all of a sudden I got there and I saw all these people in the stadium and I felt the weight."

In her upcoming album, as yet untitled, Joan wrote a song, called "A Hundred Feet Away," about a girl on the street who longs for the rock star in the penthouse. The scene shifts to the penthouse where the star paces the huge space trapped in his own isolation and loneliness. "She loves to perform but there's a price she pays for it," said Bloom. "She can't establish any close relationships. The person in that song who is Joan is not the person on the sidewalk. It's the star who's isolated from the people who actually love her. She pays that price and she feels it, but you'd never know that if she didn't write a song about it, because she so much enjoys what she's doing."

"I really want to establish myself as having done something important," Joan explains. "That's what means most to me—the history of it, the fact that I get letters all the time from fourteen- and fifteen-year-old girls saying they've picked up guitars, that they've started a band thanks to us, that they've gotten gigs. We've changed their lives. They look at me and say, 'If she can do it, I can do it.'

"I just want people to know I was here and I tried. People put so much emphasis on the fact that it's a girl singing rock 'n' roll. Why not just a *person* singing rock 'n' roll that's good? I want to get to the point where it doesn't matter. I can see it; I just don't know if I can get to it. I think I can if I've got the energy; if I can stand it for years and years and years, I think I'll get there. That's the battle. That would be the ultimate goal for me. If when people listened to my music, they loved it and didn't care if it was a guy or a girl who was singing."

Tod Frye

Photo by David Staugas

Scribbled at the bottom of a Pac-Man™ poster that hangs in Atari headquarters in Sunnyvale, California, is the question—"Why Frye?" The question refers to Tod Frye, the twenty-six-year-old high-school dropout and former hippie panhandler who transformed one of the most popular of all arcade games into a home video cassette that sold several million copies and earned him almost $1 million in royalties.

If a vote had been taken among his fellow programmers at Atari, Tod would most likely have been elected least likely to succeed. He was reprimanded for turning in a previous game late and sloppy. "When I started Pac-Man, I was one of the lowest paid programmers there. I wasn't necessarily the lowest performing. I wasn't necessarily the least competent. Actually I may have been the lowest performing," said Tod, who sometimes engages in dialogues with himself.

The only thing he seemed to excel at was behaving strangely. He earned the nickname "Arfman," for his curious habit of barking like a dog as he traveled along the company's corridors. And he bronzed his image as a wacko when he suffered his "sprinkler lobotomy." Tod was literally walking the walls one afternoon—he discovered a way to wedge his body between two walls of a narrow hallway and to shimmy along it. He was proceeding at record pace—until he smashed into a ceiling sprinkler. Tod got a free ride in an ambulance and several stitches. He was almost fired. "They said, 'Look, you're probably a real good programmer but you're not putting out.' And I buckled down."

But to those who knew him best, Tod's success came as no surprise, and the wild behavior was the best clue to his ability. "He's done a lot of pushing the limits," said Elise White, the woman whose been a surrogate mother to Tod since his own mother died when he was twelve. "The thing that makes him different from many people is his positive approach to unknowns. Most men will tell you very quickly why an idea that is a bit crazy is no good and will say, 'You can't do that because . . . .' Tod takes exactly the opposite tack, which is to quickly try to see the merit in it and then to start hunting for ways to enable the idea to succeed."

"He's always been embarrassingly good at the things he's done," added Stephen White, Elise's son, and one of Tod's oldest friends. "He starved for a while and was a hippie scumbag and was quite good at it. He went from being a ditchdigger for a carpenter here in the Bay area to being his number two man in a couple of months. He used to be able to crank the work out, producing twice as much on a daily basis as the other guys on the crew."

"I knew I could make it," said Tod, brazen as always. "I was a burnout, but I was a very bright burnout from the start."

The Oakland house Tod shares with a roommate who is a fellow Atari programmer combines elements of a 1960s crash pad and the home of the future. Tod's bedroom looks like it was hit by a meteorite. There are beer cans, dollar bills, and books everywhere. Dostoevski's *Notes from Underground* rests on Tod's never-made bed next to *Improvising Jazz Bass.*

Tod fancies himself a future David Bowie or Elvis Costello. Last year, in addition to a ranch in New Mexico and many more ephemeral investments, he bought fifteen vintage guitars. He also backed a record by a San Francisco rock group on the VOB label (Victims of Biology) and is himself the author of such would-be anthems as "Brain Damaged Baby/Comatose Cutey" and "Android Mind Police."

The room next to Tod's bedroom looks like the cockpit of the Space Shuttle. It is filled floor-to-ceiling with computer terminals and printers. Some of them belong to Tod and some of them belong to Atari. Tod owns five personal computers, including a couple that sit in the trunks of his Alfa Romeos should he get the urge to program on the road, presumably not while he's driving.

Tod has no specific schedule or workplace. He sometimes goes for weeks without visiting Sunnyvale. He can work wherever there's an electrical outlet to plug in his computer. "I don't have a normal schedule, but I'm trying to create one," he said. "When I was doing Pac-Man, it took eight months and I used to work until three or four in the morning every day. Now it's getting a lot closer to up by nine, to bed by twelve."

Tod still works more according to when his muse beckons than when the sun shines. He worked day and night throughout a recent weekend to find the solution to another arcade game. "He will totally miss important bills because he's busy tripping-off about some new programming technique," said Andy Fuchs, a friend of Tod's from high school who also works at Atari. "He'll dream programese. A lot of times he can't be bothered by regular life."

Tod inserts a Pac-Man cassette into a video player, and Pac-Man appears on the screen devouring dots with ghosts in hot pursuit. Transforming an arcade game into a home cartridge is more of an accomplishment than it might seem. It's equivalent to translating a feature length film into a three-minute cartoon without losing any of the thrill. Arcade games cost thousands of dollars and are filled with sophisticated electronics. Home games cost only a couple of hundred dollars and have proportionately less capability. "The game has to be scaled down quite a bit," Tod explained, maneuvering Pac-Man through the maze. "It's an abstraction process. I have to identify what it is that characterizes Pac-Man. I believed Pac-Man was characterized by a set of objects called ghosts chasing the little Pac-Man. There's no other word for that. It's an abstraction, a new concept. Wacka, Wacka, Wacka."

Tod's thought processes are similar to Pac-Man's movements. Occasionally he goes off the screen altogether only to reappear in a completely different place without any loss of momentum. Collecting his thoughts for publication requires some editing. He speaks in sentence fragments, facial expressions, and sounds that would make a dolphin nod knowingly. "The thing that comes to mind when you try to sum up Tod is his use of the language," Stephen White observed. "He's like a little kid playing with a new toy."

Tod plays Pac-Man proficiently but without virtuosity. "I never have time to get good at my games," he said. "I'm much more interested in going on and writing the next game."

"I know a lot of people like it and a lot of people don't like it," he commented, responding to video critics who said the Atari Pac-Man was a poor implementation of the arcade game. "The Pac-man was chunky. The ghosts flicker. I didn't want to write a game with flicker but I finally decided I didn't think the flicker would detract that much. Hell, ghosts are diaphanous anyway, right?"

Tod has gotten distracted in his defense of the game, and a ghost stuns Pac-Man. The little creature emits an electronic scream. "I know it's a good cartridge because during the summer this girl told me she had played Pac-Man to 100,000. She was too pretty to be that bored. She was a smart person who liked the game because there was some meat to it somewhere."

Others would agree with her. Pac-Man has sold over three million cartridges to make it one of the best selling of all video games. Last March Tod received a quarterly royalty check for $300,000. A year later Pac-Man is still making him $50,000 every four months.

One would expect Tod's sudden success to create some animosity among his programming peers. Yet, several are lounging in the sun on the steps in front of his house, slowly gathering the energy to attack their own terminals. There were times last year when Tod was spending as much in a day as they made in a year. On top of that, Tod isn't exactly Mr. Humility. "Andrew told a mutual acquaintance that he always knew I had it in me, that he knew I was brilliant, which I probably am," Tod said.

If there is animosity, it is tempered by the acknowledgment of his peers that Tod is too eccentric to be judged by everyday standards of etiquette. "He comes across as really arrogant sometimes, because he's really insecure, and he keeps trying to say, 'Look, I'm great, I'm wonderful,'" Andy explained. "But he's always been a real natural at logic. He's able to visualize things in an abstract way. He comes up with more original work and totally new techniques than anyone else in the department."

When Tod visited a Berkeley video store recently and saw one of his cassettes on sale, he couldn't help buying it and informing the cashier he'd written it. But despite his arrogance, he transmits genuine warmth. He has a weathered face, which makes him look older than his age, and a walrus moustache. His voice quivers when he discusses the price his instant fortune has cost him.

"Andy said that I'm rude a lot. And sometimes I may be overbearing. There were times last year when I was lost. I'd just gotten a check for a quarter of a million dollars, and I was spending sixty hours a week in the office busting ass. There was self-destructiveness. There was also sheer confusion. I was overwhelmed. I went out and bought a suit and a shirt and I got these $200 cufflinks, and there are still people being repressed in El Salvador. And I drive my Alfa Romeo and I say, It's not this easy. I've been real hungry."

Tod squandered a lot of money, but he also gave $10,000 to the Berkeley free food co-op for which he once panhandled, and a $100,000 endowment in his mother's name to the Center for Women and Religion. The center held a ceremony in Tod's honor but, in typical fashion, he never showed up.

"There was a traffic jam on the highway," Tod explains unconvincingly.

"Even if there hadn't been a traffic jam you wouldn't have gone," Andy rebuts. Tod just shrugs his shoulders.

Andy attributes Tod's abysmal manners to selfishness— on the day of the ceremony he was probably solving some programming puzzle and couldn't be bothered. In the special slang the programmers use to communicate with each other, Tod's performance was "charred."

"Most of the people who think I'm rude have never had to put up with the influences that I have," Tod said. His mother died of a long illness when he was twelve. "I was pretty brutal to my feelings," he remembers. "I spent a certain amount of time alienating them, partly with intellect. It cost me a lot of emotional repression not to care much when my Mom died."

Tod and his four brothers were raised by their father, Charles Madison Frye, who the boys called "C.M." Their relationship with him was like that of vice-presidents towards the chairman of the board. "It was an intensely competitive environment," Stephen White said. "All his sons are real intelligent and Tod's father has a big thing about that. If they weren't making the grade, it was like destructive criticism. It wasn't a supportive environment. His sons all got booted at eighteen. They were expected to sink or swim."

Tod didn't give his father a lot to be proud of. He excelled in only two areas—computers and drugs. At Berkeley High School, he had a computer class at eight in the morning and another at two in the afternoon. In between, instead of attending his other classes, he hid in a closet and played with a Wang 3300, taking time out only for lunch and to smoke an occasional joint. "I'm sort of a disciplinary problem," he admits. "I have a hard time with homework. I have a hard time with paying my taxes. It probably has something to do with father figures and authority trips."

Tod dropped out of high school during his junior year. His father mistakenly assumed that if he kicked him out of the house, Tod would shape up. "I slept in the bushes in Berkeley," he said. "A friend's family had a rundown garage that was full of leaves, and I cleaned the dry corner of that out and stayed there one rainy season. I was sort of degenerate. I was fully disenfranchised."

He panhandled for the Berkeley free food co-op which allowed him to keep 30 percent of the take. On his last day working for them, he stole the entire contents of the can, "which is really low," he admits. "I was compulsive. It was a rejection of authority, one of my fortes."

But Tod was never your average lowlife. If there was a lot of Timothy Leary about him, there was also a little Gordon Liddy. He can denounce U.S. foreign policy in the same breath that he can praise Atari for giving him an opportunity to live the American Dream; he relishes telling his hair-raising adventures, yet is looking forward to marrying Stephen White's sister, to whom he's engaged, and having kids; he can list the ways he's tried to destroy himself and then turn around and speak of future societies living off the land with high-technology.

"He has a very conservative streak in him. He's basically an extremist," Stephen White explained. "A good example is in driving. Most people kind of putt along because they've never really learned to use a car at its limits, and they're kind of afraid to. He's not made that way. He tends to learn about things by exceeding the limits in a situation and relying on his innate ability to survive. He's a natural extremist, and he occupies both extremes simultaneously without being in the middle."

Tod claims to have calmed down. He hasn't taken acid in eight years. "There are really powerful modes of perception you can go through with or without drugs," he said. "I don't use acid anymore because I have already experienced the perspective I can get by chemically altering my viewpoint, and I want to get a perspective I manifest organically. Actually, I use silicon for it. My visions are etched in ROM (Read Only Memory) [the technical term for game cartridges] and sold in multiple millions."

"I'm very willful in some ways," he muses. "Not long after my mother died I blew up a tube of glass in my hand, and I've still got many pieces of glass embedded in it. There's a constant pain that adds up to a psychological pressure. What is characteristic of me is that for as long as I could, I was a carpenter and I held my hammer in my right hand and it hurt. That's weird. So I'm a twisted individual."

SwordQuest™, the four-cartridge videogame that Tod invented and is currently programming, is infinitely more

complicated than Pac-Man. Unlike the minimalistic Pac-
Man who merely moves through a maze, the protagonists in
SwordQuest are identical twins who embark on a pilgrim-
age for a magical sword that takes them through four
worlds—Earth, Air, Fire, and Water worlds—where they encounter a variety of challenges that transform them from
rogues into wizards.

True to Tod's own nature the game exists on several levels. The theme of each cartridge is based on a different arch-
etypal image—the zodiac, the cabala, the Hindu chakras,
and the I Ching. There are also comic books that go along
with the game for people who still read a little. And there's
an actual jeweled sword worth $50,000 to be won by guess-
ing its location through clues revealed while playing the
game. "It's grandiose," Tod admits.

Tod enjoys playing video games only slightly less than in-
venting them. The arcade version of Defender is his personal favorite. "I believe videogames are good," he said.
"They teach abstraction, identification, conceptualization. I
think they're particularly good for kids because they're in-
teractive."

Frye is critical of those who contend videogames are cor-
roding the minds, morals, and eyesight of a generation of
young Americans. "It's really not fair to say that learning to
shoot planes out of the sky on a television screen will make
it any easier for people to shoot planes out of the sky for
real. I read spy novels and mysteries but I'm not a detective.

"There may be a fear that by controlling things electron-
ically, they won't identify with the results. Hell, people have
already done that with corporations. Corporate executives
do things with toxic wastes; there's the whole baby food trip
in the third world. People have removed themselves from
the consequences of their actions. So there's no reason to
think videogames will do so any more than has been done
before. I think that what they do is they teach a sense of
involvement."

Much of the time though, Tod has more practical things
on his mind than the morals of American youth. He's worried that his success with Pac-Man may have been a fluke,
and he'll never be able to repeat it. "I don't even know if I'm a
successful young American," he laughs. "I tend to be op-

timistic. I hope that I can make between $300,000 and $500,000 in 1983. It gets complicated. I mean it's a hard act to follow because there was an awful lot of luck in Pac-Man."

Tod was initially given the assignment because a bunch of more senior programmers had left the company at the same time and because his bosses didn't suspect how successful the game would become. Tod's friends believe there may have been luck in landing the assignment, but not in its execution. "Now he's really hot," said Andy Fuchs. "He's got a whole new type of logic he's putting in the computer that has not been accomplished before. He was going to try to do a videogame with a certain set of compromises, but he hit upon a way to do undoable things without the compromises."

"He's got an excellent grasp of spatial relationships," said Stephen White who saw Tod apply his algebraic abilities to carpentry. "He could do things like look at a deck and figure out the best way to arrange the boards so that you wound up cutting the fewest possible."

"I want to be an artist," Tod announced with typical bravado. "I want to make a couple of million bucks, buy a big computer that does color graphics and maybe audio, and I want to sit down and work out things that people have never been able to do before. I want to learn to express my visions as mobile four-dimensional objects with audio and graphics."

Tod said he is not disturbed the video game boom appears to be over. "When it gets down to it I really don't need to be a millionaire," he adds. "If I come out of all this a sane person with a ranch, I'll be ahead of the game."

If all else fails Tod can take his fifteen guitars and become a rock star. "I have the fundamentals," he explained. "There's something that tells me I could be great at it."

One of Tod's future projects is to transform his song "Android Mind Police" into a videogame . . . after he works out a couple of kinks. "I can't decide whether I want the androids to win or the people to win," he said, and then paused to ponder the problem. "Actually," he continued, after a while, "I think I'd like the people to win."